D0948741

Collective Decision Making

An Economic Outlook

Collective Decision Making

An Economic Outlook

SHMUEL NITZAN
and
JACOB PAROUSH

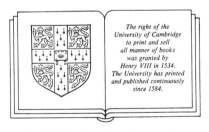

The right of the
University of Cambridge
to print and sell
all manner of books
was granted by
Henry VIII in 1534.
The University has printed
and published continuously
since 1584.

CAMBRIDGE UNIVERSITY PRESS

Cambridge
London New York New Rochelle
Melbourne Sydney

Published by the Press Syndicate of the University of Cambridge
The Pitt Building, Trumpington Street, Cambridge CB2 1RP
32 East 57th Street, New York, NY 10022, USA
10 Stamford Road, Oakleigh, Melbourne 3166, Australia

First published 1985

Printed in Great Britain at the University Press, Cambridge

Library of Congress catalogue card number: 85–5716

British Library Cataloguing in Publication Data:

Nitzan, Shmuel
Collective decision making: an economic outlook
1. Social choice   2. Economics
I. Title II. Paroush, Jacob
330'.01   HB199

ISBN 0 521 30326 5

TM

Contents

Preface

The primary purpose of this monograph is to explore the economic implications of a simple decision theoretic approach to collective choice. The classical social theoretic approach is motivated by the democratic premise that social policy, group choice or collective action should be based on the usually diverse preferences of the individuals in the society, group or collective.

In contrast, the framework adopted in the current work, the uncertain dichotomous choice model, hinges upon the alternative premise that group decision making should be based on the common objective function (preferences) of the decision makers as well as on their decisional competences.

The introductory chapter outlines the plan of the study, provides a brief historical account of the basic model, relates the current work to alternative approaches and points to some of its economic implications and applications. The bulk of the text is then divided into three parts.

Chapter 2, constituting the first part, presents the basic uncertain dichotomous choice framework. Within this framework the following two major issues are dealt with: First, the optimal decision procedure for a decision-making body. Second, the characteristics of potentially optimal decision rules. The second part comprises Chapters 3–9. In these chapters the assumptions of the basic model are successively relaxed. The effect of the respective generalizations on the optimal decision-making mechanism for the group is analyzed and their relevance to various economic issues is discussed. The third part, Chapter 10, concludes with three direct applications of the approach within the spheres of economics, medicine and law.

Each of the Chapters 3 through 10 can be read independently in conjunction with Chapter 2. Chapter 1 can be read independently. We hope, however, that this chapter stimulates the reader's interest in the following chapter and at least in some of the issues dealt with in the subsequent parts.

The methods of analysis, concepts and issues dealt with are related and relevant to many fields (notably economics, business administration, management and political science). It seems to us that this monograph is appropriate to use for short special courses (for example, in-service courses in management) or as supplementary reading matter in a variety of courses, at both the undergraduate and graduate levels, such as public choice, theory of the firm, industrial organization, labor economics, voting theory, political methodology and operations research.

Advanced mathematics is not required for the reading of this monograph. However, a modest knowledge of elementary set theory, calculus and probability theory is a useful prerequisite. Some familiarity with linear algebra is required for the Appendix to Chapter 2.

The monograph synthesizes the results of our joint research in the field over the past five years. Some of this work has been presented in eleven papers (see Paroush, 1985; Nitzan and Paroush, 1980, 1981, 1982, 1983, 1984a, 1984b, 1984c, 1984d, 1984e, and Nitzan and Procaccia, 1982). We are grateful to the publishers of the first ten of these works for the permission to republish the material contained in them. We also express our gratitude to Peter Aranson, Jim Friedman, Elon Khohlberg, Bezalel Peleg, Micha Perles, Ariel Rubinstein and Yitzhak Venezia, all of whom made useful suggestions for improvements on various parts of this work. We are especially indebted to Dr. E. Kaplinski and the staff of the Department of Cardiology, Meir Hospital, Kfar Saba, Israel, for their help in providing data for the medical application of Chapter 10. Our thanks also go to Drora Karotkine for her assistance in the computations for Tables 5.2 and 5.3, to Paula Sonnenshein for her editorial assistance with the Introduction and to Professor Uriel Procaccia for the permission to include his joint work with the first author in Section 10.3.

CHAPTER 1

Introduction

The motivation to engage in the study of judgemental aggregation procedures, viewed here as a sub-field of collective decision making, emerged a few years ago when the authors became involved in the question 'is a small body of experts more likely to make correct decisions than a large group of, not necessarily, professionals?' It soon became evident that this 'simple' question embodies a host of issues, which have held our attention ever since. Some of these issues, which were already addressed 200 years ago, have recently benefited from the contributions of scholars in various disciplines in the social sciences. Although the subject is far from exhausted, we have reached a point in our studies which, to our mind, justifies a presentation of our findings to date. The intention of the current monograph is to acquaint the reader with a systematic approach that will equip him with tools that may be helpful in gaining insight into, and solve a variety of problems related to, collective decision making. Some such problems are listed below:

(1) A group of people faces a critical choice. Should they apply a simple majority rule, or abide by a weighted rule based on individual expertise? And if the latter is utilized, what are the appropriate weights?
(2) What are the factors to be taken into account when determining the optimal size of decision-making bodies, such as academic committees, or corporate boards? How should that size be calculated?
(3) Confronted with a 'yes' or 'no' decision, what is the optimal consultation scheme for a patient; how many doctors should he consult, and how should he reach a decision when opinions diverge?
(4) Should decision makers rigidly adhere to a single rule, or allow flexibility in utilization of different decision-making rules?
(5) What is the effect of the operating costs of different rules and of the net benefit associated with correct decisions on the optimal choice of the collective decision mechanism?

(6) Certain resources are available to improve individual decision makers' skills. How ought the resources to be allocated? Should the investment in human capital be exclusively directed toward the experts, should the allocation include the less qualified, or should the latter only be the beneficiaries?
(7) A firm in a consulting industry is being established. What organizational pattern should it adopt? For example, is partnership the desirable arrangement; and if so, what is the optimal number of partners?
(8) The pattern of interdependence of decisions is, to a large extent, under the control of the designers of the collective decision-making mechanism. For example, secret voting is more likely to lessen such interdependence. Should interdependence be encouraged, or not?
(9) Is the qualified majority rule a desirable system? If so, what is the particular optimal qualified majority needed?

The study of decision making has yielded fruitful applications in many disciplines. An important distinction between the areas benefiting from decision theory is based on the level of the unit chosen for analysis; while certain disciplines focus on the individual, others deal with group decision making. The current work is an application of decision theory, where the level of the unit chosen for analysis is a group of individuals.

Decision making of the individual is affected by the amount of relevant information available to him, by his ability to utilize this information and by his personal tastes or preferences regarding the possible courses of action confronting him. Group decision making is therefore far more complicated, for a group is comprised of subjects whose individual interests may conflict and whose information and skills might differ. Such collective decisions make up a central part in several fields of economics such as public finance, welfare economics and public choice.

In a team, all members have the same interest, but they do not necessarily share the same information. In this context the central issue is how the tasks of providing information and allocating it among the decision makers should be determined. Marshack and Radner (1972) give details of a seminal study of the economic theory of teams. In organizations, control, and sometimes even identification of the information structure, might not be feasible. The current study focuses on situations where the information structure is not amenable to explicit modeling. It is assumed here that, as in a team, individual members of a group share a common interest; they are all involved in the same single task (they face the same set of possible actions), but they might possess different decisional skills. This diversity of decisional competence may partly reflect the different signals of information available to the concerned individuals. However, it is also possible that, although sharing identical information, they will reach varying decisions due to the diversity in their talents to absorb, process and translate the information into the desirable decision. For instance, consider a group of judges exposed to the very same evidence but reaching different conclusions due to their personal interpretation of the evidence and heterogeneity of their capabilities. The same phenomenon occurs with panels of medical experts who, studying the results of the same series of tests performed on a patient, may each propose a different diagnosis. Within such groups the problem is to attain the decision that will optimally utilize the decisional resources of its members.

The assumption of homogeneous preferences, a cornerstone of our decision theory approach to collective choice also differentiates our approach from the traditional social choice theory. The latter treats of the determination of desirable collective choice, given diverse individual preferences (Arrow, 1963; Sen, 1970, 1977). Classical social choice and welfare economics are to a large extent concerned with the problems of preference aggregation. Our decision theory framework focuses on the 'aggregation' of decisional skills. The heterogeneity of skills, rather than of tastes, retains the viability of the optimal group decision-making issue. Furthermore, whereas social choice usually treats problems with three or more alternatives, we concentrate on the dichotomous choice situations. Specifically, we are concerned with the problem of selecting an optimal decision rule for a group of individuals with identical objectives but, possibly, with different abilities to identify the correct course of action necessary for the attainment of their common goal. Heterogeneous preferences and multiple alternatives are the characteristic assumptions in the social choice literature; here, the problem of preference aggregation typically leads to 'impossibility theorems', or negative results, which certainly do not terminate in the identification of 'optimal' collective choice. In our model, the homogeneous preferences and binary choice assumptions, although quite restrictive, terminate in the identification of optimal collective decision rules, providing insight into the resolution of numerous realistic issues. We do not offer an alternative approach to the classical problematics of social choice theory, rather we discuss a different problem of decisional skills aggregation.

To elucidate the nature of such problems, consider the following examples:

(1) A certain firm is divided into three major departments – production, marketing, personnel – its management being composed of the three departmental heads concerned. While there is no conflict of interest among the board members, all agreeing upon the objectives of the firm, their abilities to select the correct action in order to achieve their common goal might differ. What is the optimal decision rule for such a board? Should decisions be left to the head of the relevant department (the expert rule) or should the board adopt some other strategy, e.g. decision by simple majority rule?

(2) A person, having been advised of radical surgery as a possible mode of treatment, searches for the optimal consultation scheme. He might wonder as to the most desirable strategy to determine the necessity of the operation. Should he accept the advice of the most qualified physician or consult a panel of doctors and only then apply a certain decision procedure – possibly, simple majority rule?

The approach in the current study resembles that of Condorcet (1785) and Poisson (1837) and their more recent followers Black (1948, 1958), Gelfand and Solomon (1973, 1975), Grofman (1975, 1978), Grofman *et al.* (1983) and Klevorick and Rothschild (1979). A comprehensive review of the studies deriving from the Condorcet tradition is available in Grofman (1975) and Grofman *et al.* (1983). However, our study is distinctive from all these works in that it provides a tractable analytical framework primarily designed for the purpose of facilitating the task of exploring the economics of group decision making. The effect of economic factors such as decision-making costs, shadow prices of decision rules and net benefit of correct choice on optimal group decision making are some of the issues that can be directly dealt with, utilizing our suggested framework of analysis. The effect of uncertainty regarding individual decisional skills and of interdependence among individual decisions upon collective decision making can also be analyzed within our conceptual set-up. Certain economic problems can be tackled by applying the multi-person choice framework. For example, the issue of optimal organization of industries, or that of optimal investment in human capital come to mind.

Finally, the topic treated in this essay is obliquely related to the probability aggregation problem, i.e. aggregating expert judgements regarding the probability of possible states of the world (Morris, 1974, 1977, 1983; Bordley, 1982; Madansky, 1978). In both cases, individual decision makers may share identical objectives, their judgement reflecting their proficiency. Nevertheless, the problems associated with the aggregation of probabilistic judgement resemble those of preference aggregation (Barrett and Pattanaik, 1983).

Throughout the present treatise we are mainly concerned with dichotomous choices (Bartoszynski, 1972; Fishburn and Gehrlein, 1977*b*; May, 1952). Within groups (panels of experts, boards of managers, juries, courts or committees) we consider schemes of decisions whereby each member of the group is required to opt for one of two available alternatives. In turn, we concentrate on binary collective decision rules which select one of two available choices. We characterize personal decisional skills by the individual's probabilities of making a choice that is consistent with the group objective. The members of the group share a common system of norms, all preferring the alternative that best fits their purpose. That alternative is referred to as the correct choice or the correct course of action.

The first part of the monograph deals mainly with the selection of the 'best collective decision rule'. There are several possible criteria in the light of which the search for the optimal rule within the heterogeneous preference context can be pursued. For instance, Rae (1969) suggests that a best decision rule should maximize the probability of a collective decision coinciding with any individual decision. More recently, Straffin (1977) defines a best decision rule as one which maximizes the average probability of individual decisions agreeing with the collective decision. Fishburn and Gehrlein (1977a) propose that the best decision rule should maximize expected voters' satisfaction, using yet another measure for this. Within the confines of our presumptions about the homogeneous nature of the decision-making body, we can refer to the common utility of the group members as to group utility. Therefore, a natural criterion emerges, namely we propose to define the best decision rule as that which maximizes the expected utility of the group. The collective benefit associated with the two alternatives, the size of the decision-making body, the competence of the group members and the cost inherent in the utilization of the various collective decision rules are the basic parameters of the optimization problem the group encounters. The control variable of the group problem is an element in a feasible set of collective decision rules.

The description of the basic uncertain dichotomous model is set forth in Chapter 2. This fundamental chapter simplifies matters by, first, ignoring interdependence among individual decisions, second, neglecting the possible existence of decision making costs and, finally, by assuming that the two alternatives the group faces are symmetric. Symmetry is defined as having two components. First, the label of an alternative does not convey any indication as to which of the two alternatives is the correct one, and so, a priori, the choice of either alternative is considered correct with equal probability. Second, the net benefit associated with a correct choice is independent of the labeling of the alternatives. Such symmetry justifies our focusing on neutral decision rules, in other words, rules that do not discriminate against alternatives on labeling grounds. The main result in this chapter specifies the optimal decision rule for the group, i.e. the decision rule that maximizes the expected utility of the decision makers. The optimal rule turns out to be a weighted majority rule and the explicit expression of the individual weight is given in terms of the individual's ability. This main result offers direct insight into various decisional issues. For example, it provides the necessary and sufficient conditions for the optimality of the widely-used expert rule under which group will is subordinated to the decision of the most competent individual. This result also generates conditions for optimal decisions which utilize only some of the available decisional resources and specifies sufficient conditions for the superiority of the common simple majority rule. The remainder of Chapter 2 is devoted to a close look at the set of potentially optimal decision-making rules.

In particular, we present the axiomatic characterization of weighted majority rules and discuss their efficiency merits.

Chapter 3 extends the basic model to account for typical economic considerations. Within this more general framework, net benefit of alternative decisions and direct and indirect costs of decision making associated with various possible rules are factors that play a significant role in solving the group's problems of determining the optimal collective decision rule. When the group consists of equally skilled members, and costs depend merely on the size of the decision-making body, the problem is reduced to determining optimal group size.

The economic implications of the more general situation of heterogeneous decision makers are then illustrated within the context of consulting. The analysis offers an interesting explanation regarding the structural form of consulting bodies and, to take another example, it suggests an argument questioning the efficiency of a tender system that is very common in certain business enterprises. The chapter proceeds with discussion of two particular instances of decision-making costs: the case of prohibitive costs and that of indirect costs resulting from potential variability of the individual decisional skills. In the former, we analyze the possible ranking of the relevant decision rules for small panels of experts. The ranking is based on the performance of the rules as measured by their probability of yielding the desirable collective choice. With regard to the latter, we view various forms of skill depreciation (due, for example, to health or personal problems, industrial sabotage or absenteeism) and discuss their possible costs and effects on the solution of the problem confronting the group.

Chapter 4 discusses two forms of asymmetry between the alternatives: there exist two kinds of bias in favour of one of the alternatives, e.g. the typical inclination towards the status quo. The optimal collective decision rule under these forms of asymmetry is a 'weighted qualified majority rule'. A possible formal justification for the widely-used qualified majority rules emerges. It is shown that whenever voters are equally skilled, such rules are optimal. The specific optimal qualified majority rule for equally skilled individuals depends on the size of the group, the proficiency of the decision makers and the a priori bias in favour of the status quo. The interrelationships among these three parameters are analyzed and illustrated in the concluding section of the chapter. These interrelationships have significant implications for the theory of democratic constitutional design.

It is difficult to pursue a meaningful discussion of decision making without dealing with the topic of uncertainty. Uncertainty pervades the structure of decision problems, the procedures for taking decisions, preferences over the alternatives and knowledge affecting outcome, as well as the very structure of organizations. The representation of decisional skills via the individual probabilities of judging correctly, directly reveals the particular role uncertainty plays in our dichotomous choice models. Admittedly, a major drawback of the optimality analysis based on these models is that it is predicated on probabilistic values which are usually unknown. Chapter 5 extends the optimality analysis to some examples of incomplete information on decisional skills. Thus, an additional dose of uncertainty is explicitly injected into the basic uncertain dichotomous choice model by relaxing the full information assumption regarding the competence of the decision makers. Two possible forms of incomplete information are discussed. In the first case, there exists some direct partial information on decisional skills and in the second, some information is available regarding the distribution of decisional competences in the population from which the decision makers are drawn. The evaluation of decision rules (some, or all, of the relevant rules) is then carried out under alternative forms of incomplete information on individual decisional competence.

Chapter 6 deals with three major issues. How can the widely recognized phenomenon of interdependence among individual decisions be explicitly incorporated into the basic dichotomous choice model? Can we, by replacing the independence assumption with an operational dependence pattern, identify the optimal decision rule for the group? In particular, what can be salvaged from the optimality result under independent voting for the different and more realistic circumstances where choices are interrelated? And lastly, assuming that the second issue cannot be satisfactorily resolved, is it still possible to accomplish the more modest task of comparing the group performance under the alternative independent and interdependent patterns?

Starting with the conceptual challenge, we have deliberately confined our discussion to situations where individual actual decisions are neutrally dependent on own views and on the views of others (interdependence is invariant to labeling of the alternatives). It is then shown that the optimal group performance under interdependent voting can only be adversely affected by any pattern of interaction. In particular, the optimal rule corresponding to such a pattern cannot be superior to the optimal rule under the basic model described in Chapter 2.

In the earlier chapters, individual decisional skills are considered to be exogenous parameters, whether estimated, known, partially known or unknown. Chapter 7 generalizes the basic model in treating the individual competences as endogenously determined variables. However, the scope of the analysis in this chapter is somewhat limited, since it is carried out under the assumption that group decisions are obtained using the common simple majority rule. Individual decisional competence can now be varied through investment in human capital. Members of the group are therefore represented by a common production function which relates amount of investment to the individual decisional skill. We first analyze the individual's investment problem and then address the social human capital allocation problem. The analysis clarifies the relationship between optimal investment in human capital, net social benefit of correct decisions and the size of the decision-making body. It also enables comparison between the total volume of investment in the centralized system (the democratic multi-person collective choice model) and the total investment in human capital in an alternative decentralized equivalent system.

Chapter 8 generalizes the basic model by extending the set of feasible decision rules. Instead of concentrating on deterministic collective decision rules, it allows for sequential decision processes. That is, given the actual choices of k individuals, the more general collective decision rules may select one of the available alternatives or they might choose to introduce new relevant information by resorting to the views of additional decision makers. Here, group size is neither a fixed parameter – as in the basic model – nor a control variable as in Chapter 3 (the case of heterogeneous individuals), but rather becomes a random variable. We pursue the sequential analysis using the consulting context which offers a significant natural application for this generalized form of the basic model. The optimal sequential consulting process depends on the pool of available consultants. It also depends on both the benefit of correct choice and decision-making costs of alternative rules. Therefore the sequential model further generalizes the basic model as it takes into account economic considerations which are similar to those dealt with in Chapter 3.

Three additional variations on the basic theme are briefly scanned in Chapter 9: the replacement of the pairwise choice assumption by a multiple choice context, the allowance for more general collective decision rules yielding non-deterministic probabilistic outcome and the generalization permitting both individual and social mixed strategies on the alternatives. We argue that the dichotomous choice model is of paramount importance by itself and, additionally, it is indicative of the multiple alternative case in the decision theoretic context. The discussion on the second issue establishes that generalizing the basic model by allowing collective decision rules to yield lotteries is futile. Specifically, the option to select non-deterministic decision rules will not be exploited; the group will always select a deterministic optimal rule. The chapter concludes with a brief survey of some recent studies that deal with the problem of aggregating individual probabilistic assessments as to the correctness of the available alternatives rather than aggregating the deterministic decision profiles of the individuals.

The basic uncertain dichotomous choice model and its various extensions have numerous potential applications in a variety of fields. Some of these applications are presented and scrutinized in the early chapters. Chapter 10 is wholly devoted to three more detailed applications within the areas of medicine, law and industrial organization. The medical one is concerned with the efficiency of a cardiac diagnostic system and is illustrated within a hospital setting. Estimating the decisional skills of cardiologists, we demonstrate that diagnosis by a single physician, even the most qualified one, might be inferior to diagnosis by a panel of cardiologists using a simple majority rule. In the legal application, we utilize the basic model to compare the two election methods quite regularly used by corporate boards. Under the first method, the 'common law', directors are elected to office if they carry the majority of the voting shares represented at the stockholders' general meeting. Under the second method, cumulative voting, the candidates receiving the largest number of votes are elected to the board. The third application focuses on industrial organization issues. In particular, it attempts to clarify why partnership, as a form of economic organization, is especially popular in some industries within the services sector.

Some of the assumptions of the basic uncertain dichotomous choice model are indeed necessary in order to enable the formulation of a solvable optimization problem encountered by the group. The independence assumption is a notable example. Others can be relaxed and replaced by more meaningful ones. Such is the case with the assumptions regarding the symmetric nature of the alternatives or the assumption ignoring decision-making costs. Such relaxation does not fundamentally affect the main lesson to be learned from the decision theoretic approach to collective decision making. Even for individuals sharing identical preferences there exists a meaningful social choice problem. We wish to suggest that the particular conclusions and implications derived from our analysis, although limited in scope, point to significant practical implications in numerous more relevant settings. The tip of the iceberg is useful, but there is still considerable distance between the initial applications, suggestions and implications made within a particular dichotomous choice model and a universal decision theory treating collective choice.

CHAPTER 2

Uncertain dichotomous choice: the basic model

The basic ingredients of any approach to collective decision making are a set of alternatives, a set of individuals and an aggregation procedure associating with each assignment of some individual characteristics (e.g. votes, preferences, skills or power distribution) a collective choice. This chapter opens with a detailed description of one such collective choice approach, namely the particular case which will be referred to as the basic uncertain dichotomous choice model. The main characteristics of this model are presented in the form of eight assumptions. These assumptions imply that the group faces a well-defined constrained optimization problem and they completely identify the basic components of this paradigmatic economic problem – the group objective function, the group decision variables and the feasible set of decision variables.

The solution to the problem the group faces, i.e. the identification of the optimal decision-making procedure, constitutes the main contribution of this chapter. In subsequent chapters we will be relaxing the basic assumptions and will study, among other issues, the corresponding effect on the main result. In the concluding sections of this chapter we discuss some of the implications of this optimality result and take a closer look at the set of potentially optimal decision-making rules. In particular we present the axiomatic characterization for these rules and discuss their efficiency merits.

2.1 The model

Consider a set of individuals $N = \{1, \ldots, n\}$ where n also denotes the number of elements in N, that is $|N| = n$. The set N is interpreted as a group of decision makers (a panel of experts, a board of managers, a committee, etc.) and we assume that the group and, in particular, its size are fixed. In a dichotomous choice situation the set N is required to select one of two alternatives such as 'support' or 'reject' a certain proposal, answer 'yes' or 'no' to a certain question and, in general, select alternative a or alternative b. Note that group decision making in situations involving pairwise choice is very common either in natural binary contexts (e.g. choice under critical conditions that are typically characterized by the availability of only two courses of action) or artificial binary contexts where the group faces more than two alternatives but it decomposes the decision-making process into a sequence of pairwise choices (e.g. the standard amendment legislative procedure).

Let an individual decision between a and b be represented by the variable x_i where $x_i = 1$ and $x_i = -1$ are interpreted as votes cast by individual i for alternative a and alternative b respectively. An n-tuple of such decisive (abstentions are not allowed) individual variables $x = (x_1, \ldots, x_n)$ is called a decision profile and the set of possible decision profiles is denoted by Ω. We are concerned with collective decision making which is based on the group members decisions. The study is therefore confined to a particular form of aggregation procedures that specify a unique collective choice for any possible decision profile. Formally, a decisive decision rule (DDR) f is a function from the set of all possible decision profiles to the set $\{1, -1\}$ where we interpret $f(x_1, \ldots, x_n) = 1$ and $f(x_1, \ldots, x_n) = -1$ as the group N having selected alternative a and alternative b respectively, given the profile $x = (x_1, \ldots, x_n)$ and utilizing the rule f. Ruling out individual abstentions the possibility of collectively deciding not to decide is also eliminated. This very assumption is reflected by the decisiveness of f. The set of all possible decisive decision rules is denoted by F. If $|N| = n$ then $|F| = 2^{2^n}$ where the number of elements in a set S is denoted by $|S|$.

Assume now that the members of N share the same utility U and that they are all interested in expected utility maximization. Unlike the classical social choice model, here individuals' preferences are identical and therefore all the decision makers prefer the choice of that option which best suits their common will.

We assume that one, and only one, such option exists, and refer to it as the correct decision. The other alternative is referred to as the incorrect alternative. In such a dichotomous-choice situation, however, the ability of each individual to make the correct choice, i.e. to identify which of the available alternatives is the correct one, is usually limited. This may be due to lack of skill and information, or to the uncertainty of the environment in which the situation exists. Hence, assume that there is a random variable y_i associated with individual i ($i = 1, \ldots, n$) such that

$$y_i = \begin{cases} 1 & \text{if } i \text{ selects the correct alternative} \\ -1 & \text{if } i \text{ selects the incorrect alternative} \end{cases}$$

and denote by p_i the probability that $y_i = 1$, $p_i = \Pr\{y_i = 1\}$. Abstention is ruled out and therefore $\Pr\{y_i = -1\} = 1 - p_i$. The vector $p = (p_1, \ldots, p_n)$ is called a vector of abilities or skills and with no loss of generality we let $p_i \geq p_j$ if $i < j$.

Individual decisional skills are initially assumed to be both fixed and known to the designer of the collective decision-making system. In addition, the values of p_i are assumed to be statistically independent.

We confine our attention to the case of perfectly symmetric alternatives by assuming, first, that the label of an alternative, a or b, does not convey any indication as to which of the two is the correct one. Consequently, the alternatives might be a priori considered equiprobable and the values of p_i might be interpreted as reflecting individual abilities only. Moreover, the loss (benefit) incurred by an incorrect (correct) choice is assumed to be the same, regardless of the particular alternative mistakenly (correctly) chosen.[1] Denote the benefit associated with correct and incorrect decisions respectively by B_s and B_f. Symmetry implies invariance of the model to labeling of the alternatives, and it inherently calls for the restriction of our study to neutral decisive decision rules, that is rules that do not discriminate against one of the alternatives on labeling grounds; interchanging the labels of these alternatives always results in the reversal of the collective decision.

Formally, a DDR f is neutral if, for any decision profile, $(x_1,\ldots,x_n)$, $f(-x_1,\ldots,-x_n) = -f(x_1,\ldots,x_n)$. Finally, we totally ignore, in this chapter, differences among decision rules that are based on the possibly different costs associated with the operation of the rules. This we do by assuming that the operating costs associated with any rule are identically equal to zero.

The description of the basic model is now complete. To summarize it we list below eight assumptions that relate to the three elements comprising the model; the set of alternatives, the individual decision makers and the aggregation rule.

Alternatives
Assumption 1: The set of alternatives consists of two elements a, b.
Assumption 2: The alternatives are symmetric.
(a) The alternatives are a priori equally likely to be correct.
(b) The net benefit $B = B_s - B_f$ associated with a correct choice is independent of the identity of the correct choice.

Individuals
Assumption 3: Individuals share a common utility U and they are expected utility maximizers.
Assumption 4: Individual decisional skills are represented by their fixed probabilities of making the correct judgement (the values of p_i) while confronting the available alternatives.
Assumption 5: The set N is fixed. In particular the values of p_i and n are held constant.

Assumption 6: Individual choices are independent.

The aggregation rule

Assumption 7: The aggregation procedure is a neutral, deterministic and decisive decision rule.

Assumption 8: The costs associated with any decision rule f are identically equal to zero.

2.2   The problem

Within the basic uncertain dichotomous framework an optimal decisive decision rule maximizes the expected common utility of the decision makers. Denoting by $\pi = \pi(f, p)$ the probability of obtaining a correct alternative this objective function is

$$\pi B_s + (1 - \pi)B_f = \pi(B_s - B_f) + B_f$$

where B_s and B_f are the utility levels corresponding to success and failure respectively in choosing the correct alternative. Since B_s and B_f are constants, this objective function can be further reduced to πB where $B = B_s - B_f$ is the net benefit, in utility terms, of a correct decision. Finally, since B is constant, maximizing expected utility is equivalent to the maximization of π, the collective probability of making the correct choice. Hence the problem on which we focus reduces to

(2.2.1) $\max\limits_{f \in M} \pi(f, p)$ where $M = \{ f \in F : f \text{ is neutral}\}$

That is, our optimization problem under the basic model is the selection of a neutral DDR which maximizes the probability of obtaining the correct alternative. In order to define that probability formally it is necessary to introduce two more random variables.

Consider first the n-dimensional random variable $y = (y_1, \ldots, y_n)$ and denote by $g(y) = \Pr\{Y = y\}$ the probability function defined over $\Omega = \{y = (y_1, \ldots, y_n) : y_i \in \{1, -1\}\}$.[2] Given statistical independence among the values of p_i we obtain

$$g(y) = \prod_{i \in A(y)} p_i \prod_{i \in B(y)} (1 - p_i)$$

$$\text{where } i \in \begin{cases} A(y) & \text{if } y_i = 1 \\ B(y) & \text{if } y_i = -1 \end{cases}$$

Note that

$$\sum_{y \in \Omega} g(y) = 1$$

Consider now the random variable $f(y): \Omega \rightarrow \{1, -1\}$ which is associated with a particular DDR f.

$$f(y) = \begin{cases} 1 & \text{if } f \text{ selects the correct alternative} \\ -1 & \text{if } f \text{ selects the incorrect alternative} \end{cases}$$

For instance, if f is the expert rule, i.e. $f(x) = x_1$, then $f(y) = y_1$ is the random variable associated with the expert rule. Or, if f is simple majority rule and n is odd, i.e.

$$f(x) = \text{sign} \left(\sum_{i=1}^{n} x_i \right)^3 \quad \text{then} \quad f(y) = \text{sign} \left(\sum_{i=1}^{n} y_i \right)$$

is the random variable associated with simple majority rule.

Any given neutral DDR f partitions the sample space into two mutually exclusive and exhaustive sets $Y(1, f)$ and $\Omega - Y(1, f)$ where

$$Y(1, f) = \{y : f(y) = 1\}$$

The probability of obtaining the correct alternative under the neutral DDR f is

$$\pi(f, p) = \Pr\{f(y) = 1\} = \Pr\{y \in Y(1, f)\} = \sum_{y \in Y(1, f)} g(y)$$

For instance, $\pi(f, p) = p_1$ when $f(x) = x_1$, or

$$\pi(f, p) = \sum_{j=k+1}^{n} \binom{n}{j} q^j (1-q)^{n-j}$$

when

$$f(x) = \text{sign} \left(\sum_{i=1}^{n} x_i \right), \quad n = 2k + 1$$

k is an integer and $p = (q, \ldots, q)$.

Note that solving problem (2.2.1) is fully compatible with the objective of expected utility maximization. To see this point notice that the expected benefit is

$$E = B_s \sum_{y \in Y(1, f)} g(y) + B_f \sum_{y \in \Omega - Y(1, f)} g(y)$$

and, by neutrality, this is equal to

$$B_s \sum_{y \in Y(1, f)} g(y) + B_f \left[1 - \sum_{y \in Y(1, f)} g(y) \right] = \sum_{y \in Y(1, f)} g(y) [B_s - B_f] + B_f$$

$$= \pi(f, p) [B_s - B_f] + B_f$$

2.3   The optimal decision rule

The optimal decision rule for our group N turns out to be a decisive weighted majority rule. A decisive decision rule (DDR) f is called a decisive weighted majority rule (DWMR) if it satisfies

$$f(x) = \text{sign}\left(\sum_{i=1}^{n} w_i x_i \right)$$

for every decision profile x in Ω with respect to some semi-positive[4] vector $w = (w_1, \ldots, w_n)$ for which $\Sigma w_i x_i \neq 0$ for any x in Ω. The vector w is called a system of weights. Note that any semi-positive vector of integers w, whose sum of components is odd, defines the DWMR

$$f(x) = \text{sign}\left(\sum_{i=1}^{n} w_i x_i \right)$$

Note that a DWMR can be represented by different systems of weights. More precisely, a distinct DWMR is defined in terms of a system of weights which is a representative element of an equivalent set of vectors all defining the same rule. For instance, when $n = 3$, (w_1, w_2, w_3) and (kw_1, kw_2, kw_3) define the same DWMR, where k is any positive integer, or $(1, 1, 1)$ and $(6, 7, 8)$ both define simple majority rule. In general, two systems of weights define the same rule if they imply identical structures of winning coalitions. The weights defining the DWMR that solves problem (2.2.1) are proportional to the logarithms of the individual odds of identifying the correct alternative. This is shown formally in the following theorem.

Theorem 2.3.1 The solution $\hat{f}(p)$ to problem (2.2.1) is given by

$$\hat{f}(p) = \text{sign}\left(\sum_{i=1}^{n} \beta_i x_i \right) \quad \text{where} \quad \beta_i = \ln\frac{p_i}{(1 - p_i)}[5]$$

Proof: If $f(y) = 1$ whenever $g(y) > g(-y)$, then $\text{Pr}\{y \in Y(1, f)\}$ is maximized and so f is an optimal DDR. We proceed by demonstrating that $\hat{f}$ is such a rule. For every $y \in Y(1, f)$

$$\hat{f} = \text{sign}\left(\sum_{i=1}^{n} \beta_i x_i \right)$$

implies

$$\sum_{i \in A(y)} \beta_i y_i > \sum_{j \in B(y)} \beta_j y_j$$

or equivalently

$$\prod_{i\in A(y)} \frac{p_i}{(1 - p_i)} > \prod_{j\in B(y)} \frac{p_j}{(1 - p_j)}$$

or equivalently

$$g(y) = \prod_{i\in A(y)} p_i \prod_{j\in B(y)} (1 - p_j) > \prod_{i\in A(y)} (1 - p_i) \prod_{j\in B(y)} p_j = g(-y)$$

In general, the weights defining the optimal weighted majority rule are not restricted to be non-negative. However, with no loss of generality the weights can be assumed to be non-negative since if $p_i < \frac{1}{2}$, the designer of the optimal decision system for the group N can improve the performance of individual i by consistently reversing his decision. This strategy would increase individual i's probability of making a correct choice to $(1 - p_i) > \frac{1}{2}$. Assigning a negative weight

$$\beta_i = \ln\left(\frac{p_i}{1 - p_i}\right)$$

or a positive weight

$$\ln\left(\frac{1 - p_i}{p_i}\right)$$

with consistent reversal of i's decisions are equivalent strategies that lead to the same optimal DDR. Hence, with no loss of generality, we henceforth assume that even the least competent individual is a decisional asset, that is $p_n > 0.5$.

The identification of the optimal neutral DDR for decision-making bodies of any size directly reveals under what circumstances the group decisions should be made by a committee of experts; put differently, under what circumstances some individuals should never have any effect on the collective outcome. Of course, such individuals would be the least competent members and they are fully identified by the following corollary.

Corollary 2.3.1 (1) Let

$$\beta^*(m) = \min_{x_1,\ldots,x_m}\left[\left(\sum_{i=1}^{m} \beta_i x_i\right): \sum_{i=1}^{m} \beta_i x_i \geq 0\right]$$

Then

$$\hat{f}(p) = \operatorname{sign}\left(\sum_{i=1}^{m} \beta_i x_i\right)$$

where $\bar{m}$ is the smallest m satisfying

$$\beta^*(m) > \sum_{i=m+1}^{n} \beta_i$$

Proof: It is straightforward to verify that

$$\text{sign}\left(\sum_{i=1}^{n} \beta_i x_i\right) = \text{sign}\left(\sum_{i=1}^{m} \beta_i x_i\right) \forall x \in \Omega$$

Hence, whenever $\bar{m} < n$, the optimal decision rule entirely ignores the decisions of the $(n - \bar{m})$ least-skilled individuals. That is, the optimal decision rule in such cases is, in fact, an $\bar{m}$ experts weighted majority rule.

An important special case of the above corollary is obtained when $\bar{m} = 1$. Here the commonly used expert rule ($f(x_1, \ldots, x_n) = x_1$ for any decision profile $(x_1, \ldots, x_n)$) emerges as the optimal rule. The necessary and sufficient condition for the superiority of the expert rule is given below.

Corollary 2.3.1 (2)

$$\hat{f}(p) = x_1 \quad \text{if and only if} \quad \beta_1 > \sum_{j=2}^{n} \beta_j$$

Proof: Note that $\beta^*(1) = \beta_1$. If

$$\beta_1 > \sum_{j=2}^{n} \beta_j$$

then $\bar{m} = 1$. By the previous corollary

$$\text{sign}\left(\sum_{i=1}^{n} \beta_i x_i\right) = x_1$$

The sufficient condition for the preferability of the expert rule is certainly not satisfied whenever the decision makers are sufficiently homogeneous in abilities. Under the extreme case of equally skilled individuals the optimal DDR is simple majority rule where the weights are equally distributed among all decision makers. For example, $w = (1, \ldots, 1)$ and, in turn, simple majority rule is given by

$$f(x) = \text{sign}\left(\sum_{i=1}^{n} x_i\right)$$

Corollary 2.3.1 (3) establishes that the existence of identical skills is a sufficient condition for the superiority of simple majority rule.

Corollary 2.3.1 (3)

$$\hat{f}(p) = \text{sign}\left(\sum_{i=1}^{2k+1} x_i\right) \quad \text{if} \quad p_i = p, \quad i = 1, \ldots, 2k+1$$

Proof: If $p_i = p$ for every i in N, then also $\beta_i = \beta$ for all i. In turn,

$$\text{sign}\left(\sum_{i=1}^{n} \beta_i x_i\right) = \text{sign}\left(\beta \sum_{i=1}^{n} x_i\right) = \text{sign}\left(\sum_{i=1}^{n} x_i\right)$$

The last two corollaries seem to suggest that the larger the homogeneity of decisional skills the more democratic is the optimal decision rule for the group.

2.4   Axiomatic characterization of potentially optimal decisive decision rules

The set of all DWMRs for a given group size n, $W(n)$, is the set of potentially optimal DDRs. This set is uniquely characterized by two properties: monotonicity and strong neutrality.

2.4.1 *Monotonicity*

A DDR f is monotonic if $x \geqslant x' \rightarrow f(x) \geqslant f(x')$

$\forall x, x' \in \Omega$.

That is, if a certain alternative is selected under the decision profile x', then the same alternative must win under the profile x where its status has improved, i.e. a change has occurred which only added supporters to the previously winning alternative. This property guarantees that the rule f is positively responsive to changes in the decision makers' attitudes.

2.4.2 *Strong neutrality*

A DDR f is strongly neutral if for all $m > 1$ and all $x^1, \ldots, x^m \in \Omega$

$$\sum_{j=1}^{m} x^j = 0 \rightarrow [\, f(x^j) = 1$$

for some

$$j \in \{1, \ldots, m\} \text{ iff } f(x^k) = -1 \text{ for some } k \in \{1, \ldots, m\}\,].$$

That is, for any set of decision profiles in which each individual exactly splits his decisions between the two alternatives, strong neutrality requires that each of the alternatives is chosen collectively under at least one decision profile. Put differently, consider a sequence of decision profiles $x^1, \ldots, x^m$ in which each i casts exactly as many votes for alternative a as he does for alternative b. Strong neutrality requires that one alternative is the collective outcome under at least one profile iff the other alternative is the collective outcome under at least one profile.

The axiomatic characterization of DWMRs is given by the following result.

Theorem 2.4.1 A DDR f is a DWMR iff it is monotonic and strongly neutral.

The proofs of this theorem as well as subsequent theorems in this chapter appear in the Appendix to this chapter.

The requirement of monotonicity within our model is fully justified because a rule f cannot be efficient unless it satisfies the monotonicity property (see Theorem 2.5.1 in the next section). Strong neutrality implies the standard and weaker neutrality property that is commonly used in the social choice literature and which was already explicitly introduced into the basic model (let $m = 2$ in the definition of strong neutrality to obtain the neutrality property). Unfortunately strong neutrality is a rather restrictive and not an easily justifiable property. Were it a plausible condition we could have restricted, by Theorem 2.4.1, the feasible set of DDRs in problem 2.2.1 to the set of DWMRs. Nevertheless, for decision-making bodies where $n \leqslant 5$ we do obtain that strong neutrality and neutrality are equivalent.

Theorem 2.4.2 Let $n \leqslant 5$. Then a DDR is a DWMR iff it is monotonic and neutral.[6]

The following example demonstrates that when $n = 6$ a DDR might satisfy neutrality but violate strong neutrality.

Example 2.4.1 Partition Ω (the set of all possible voting profiles) into the three sets

$$\Omega^+ = \left\{ x \in \Omega : \sum_{i=1}^{6} x_i > 0 \right\}$$

$$\Omega^- = \left\{ x \in \Omega : \sum_{i=1}^{6} x_i < 0 \right\}$$

$$\Omega^0 = \left\{ x \in \Omega : \sum_{i=1}^{6} x_i = 0 \right\}$$

Now partition Ω^0 into the four sets

$$\Omega_1^0 = \{(1, -1, 1, -1, 1, -1), (1, 1, -1, -1, -1, 1),$$
$$(-1, 1, 1, 1, -1, -1), (-1, -1, -1, 1, 1, 1)\}$$

$$\Omega_2^0 = \{x \in \Omega^0: \ -x \in \Omega_1^0\}$$

$$\Omega_3^0 = \{x \in \Omega^0 - \{\Omega_1^0 \cup \Omega_2^0\}: \ x_1 = 1\}$$

$$\Omega_4^0 = \{x \in \Omega^0: \ -x \in \Omega_3^0\}$$

Finally let

$$f(x) = \begin{cases} 1, & x \in \{\Omega^+ \cup \Omega_1^0 \cup \Omega_3^0\} \\ -1, & x \in \{\Omega^- \cup \Omega_2^0 \cup \Omega_4^0\} \end{cases}$$

It can readily be verified that f is neutral, however, the sum of the four voting profiles in Ω_1^0 is zero, yet $f(x) = 1$ for all $x \in \Omega_1^0$, i.e. strong neutrality is violated.

2.5 Efficiency

A DDR f' is inefficient if there exists a DDR f such that $\pi(f, p) \geqslant \pi(f', p)$ for all ability vectors and strict inequality holds for some p. In other words, an inefficient rule can be dominated by some other rules whereas the set of efficient rules E consists of undominated rules. By Theorem 2.3.1 it is quite obvious that for any group size the set of DWMRs is a subset of the efficient DDRs, that is $W(n) \subset E(n)$. But is it also true that $W(n) = E(n)$? Is the inclusion of a decision rule in $W(n)$ a necessary and sufficient condition for being efficient? This question is very significant in situations where second best DDRs are looked for. For example, should we focus on DWMRs only when there is no information on decisional skills, when there is only partial information on individual competences or when full information regarding the skills vector p is available but there is some restriction (institutional, technical or economical) on using the first best rule?

The answer to the question whether $W(n) = E(n)$ is, in general, negative. However, for $n \leqslant 5$, the set of efficient rules coincides with the set of DWMRs.

Theorem 2.5.1 For $n \leqslant 5$, $W(n) = E(n)$.

The proof follows from Theorem 2.4.2 and the intuitive proposition that efficiency implies monotonicity (see Lemma 3 in the proof of Theorem 2.5.1 in the Appendix to this chapter). Note that requiring strong neutrality rather than neutrality in the basic model results, by Theorem 2.4.1, in the equivalence of E and W for any n. Also note that, by Theorem 2.3.1, there is a constructive way to show that if $f_0 \in W$, then there is some skill vector p^0 whose elements p_i^0 are functions of $w_i(f_0)$ for which this f_0 maximizes $\pi(f, p^0)$. In other words, every DWMR f_0 defined by a set of weights $w^0 = (w_1^0, \ldots, w_n^0)$ is optimal for the skill vector p^0 where $p^0 = \exp(w_i^0)/[1 - \exp(w_i^0)]$.

Finally we present below the set of relevant DWMRs for $n \leqslant 5$. A DDR f' is

Table 2.1

n	$W^*(n)$	$|W^*(n)|$
2	(1, 0)	1
3	(1, 0, 0), (1, 1, 1)	2
4	(1, 0, 0, 0), (2, 1, 1, 1), (1, 1, 1, 0)	3
5	(1, 0, 0, 0, 0), (1, 1, 1, 1, 1), (1, 1, 1, 0, 0)	7
	(2, 1, 1, 1, 0), (2, 2, 1, 1, 1), (3, 2, 2, 1, 1)	
	(3, 1, 1, 1, 1)	

called inefficient relative to the vector of skills p^0 if there exists a **DDR** f such that $\pi(f, p) \geqslant \pi(f', p)$ for all $p \in G(p^0)$ with strict inequality for at least some $p' \in G(p^0)$, where

$$G(p^0) = \{p : p_i > p_j \text{ if } p_i^0 > p_j^0 \text{ and } p_i = p_j \text{ if } p_i^0 = p_j^0 \text{ for all } i, j\}$$

Obviously, if f is inefficient, then it is also inefficient relative to some p. The converse is not true. A DWMR that is efficient relative to the actual vector of decisional competences of members in N is called relevant. Recall that we have assumed that individuals are ordered by their skills. Relevance of a DWMR is guaranteed by assigning weights according to skills, as specifically shown in the following theorem.

Theorem 2.5.2 A decisive weighted majority rule defined by the system of weights w is efficient relative to p^0 if $w_i \geqslant w_j$ whenever $p_i^0 > p_j^0$.

By Theorems 2.4.2 and 2.5.2, if $n = 2$, then there is only one relevant DWMR, the expert rule. If $n = 3$, then there are two relevant DWMRs: the expert rule and simple majority rule. If $n = 4$, then there are three relevant DWMRs: the expert rule, simple majority within the three most competent individuals and simple majority rule with a tie-breaking chairman (individual 1). If $n = 5$, then there are seven relevant DWMRs. The expert rule: a set of weights which defines this rule is $(1, 0, 0, 0, 0)$. Simple majority rule: a system of weights which defines this rule is $(1, 1, 1, 1, 1)$. Restricted simple majority rule defined by the system of weights $(1, 1, 1, 0, 0)$, that is decisions are obtained within the set of the three most competent individuals applying the simple majority rule. The fourth rule is a restricted simple majority rule with a tie-breaking chairman, a system of weights which defines this rule is $(2, 1, 1, 1, 0)$. The fifth rule is defined by the weights $(2, 2, 1, 1, 1)$ and is almost identical to simple majority rule, the only exception is that the three least competent decision makers do not constitute a winning coalition; put differently, a minority of the two most able individuals is decisive. The sixth rule is almost a restricted simple majority rule with the exception that the expert is decisive if the two least competent members support him; a set of weights which defines this rule is $(3, 2, 2, 1, 1)$. Finally, the seventh rule is almost an expert rule, the weights $(3, 1, 1, 1, 1)$ define this rule. The only difference between this rule and the expert rule is that here a united front of the four less able individuals enjoys a veto power. The reasonable DWMRs for small decision-making bodies $W^*(n)$, $n \leq 5$, are presented in Table 2.1.[7]

Appendix

Theorem 2.4.1 A DDR f is a DWMR iff it is monotonic and strongly neutral.

Proof:

Necessity – Suppose that f is a DWMR. Then there is a semi-positive integral vector $w = (w_1, \ldots, w_n)$ such that

$$f(x) = \text{sign} \left(\sum_{i=1}^{n} w_i x_i \right)$$

for all $x \in \Omega$. Since $w \geq 0$, the linear function

$$\sum_{i=1}^{n} w_i x_i$$

is monotonic. The sign function is monotonic and, therefore, f is monotonic (being a monotonic function of a monotonic function). In order to establish the neutrality of f, suppose that

$$\sum_{k=1}^{m} x^k = \mathbf{0}$$

i.e. $\sum_{k=1}^{m} x_i^k = 0$

for every $i = 1, \ldots, n$. For each individual i we thus get

$$\sum_{k=1}^{m} w_i x_i^k = 0$$

and hence $\sum_{k=1}^{m} \sum_{i=1}^{n} w_i x_i^k = 0$

Consider a particular voting profile $x^{k'}$ which satisfies

$$\sum_{i=1}^{n} w_i x_i^{k'} > 0$$

There must therefore exist some k'' such that

$$\sum_{i=1}^{n} w_i x_i^{k''} < 0$$

i.e. neutrality is satisfied.

Sufficiency – Suppose that f is a neutral and monotonic DDR. Let $X(1,f) = \{x \in \Omega \mid f(x) = 1\}$. By neutrality, if $X(1,f) = \{x^1, \ldots, x^{\bar{m}}\}$, $\bar{m} = 2^{n-1}$, and

$$\sum_{k=1}^{\bar{m}} \alpha_k x^k = 0$$

where $\alpha_k \geq 0$ are rational numbers, then $\alpha_k = 0 \, \forall k \in \{1, \ldots, \bar{m}\}$. Assuming that some of the rational numbers α_k were not equal to 0 we could find – by multiplication in a common denominator – a semi-positive integral vector $r = (r_1, \ldots, r_{\bar{m}})$ that satisfies

$$\sum_{k=1}^{\bar{m}} r_k x^k = \mathbf{0}$$

Using the values of r_k to generate duplicates of the profiles x^k we could then form the sequence

$$\underbrace{x^1, \ldots, x^1}_{r_1}, \underbrace{x^2, \ldots, x^2}_{r_2}, \ldots, \underbrace{x^{\bar{m}}, \ldots, x^{\bar{m}}}_{r_{\bar{m}}} = x^1, \ldots, x^m$$

where

$$m = \sum_{k=1}^{\bar{m}} r_k \quad \text{and} \quad \sum_{j=1}^{m} x^j = 0$$

The neutrality condition would have thus been violated, since $f(x^j) = 1$, $(j = 1, \ldots, m)$. This implies that $\mathbf{0}$ is an extreme point of the cone C spanned by the vectors $x^1, \ldots, x^{\bar{m}}$. Therefore, there exists a hyperplane H supporting C such that $C \cap H = \{\mathbf{0}\}$ and hence, there exists a vector $s = (s_1, \ldots, s_n)$ such that

$$\sum_{i=1}^{n} s_i \zeta_i > 0$$

for all $\mathbf{0} \neq (\zeta_1, \ldots, \zeta_n) \in C$. In particular,

$$\sum_{i=1}^{n} s_i x_i > 0 \quad \forall x \in X(1,f)$$

By neutrality, if $x \in X(1, f)$, then $-x \in \{\Omega - X(1, f)\}$ and so

$$f(x) = \text{sign}\left(\sum_{i=1}^{n} s_i x_i\right) \forall x \in \Omega$$

Let us proceed by showing that the semi-positive vector $w = (w_1, \ldots, w_n)$

$$w_i = \begin{cases} s_i & \text{if } s_i \geq 0 \\ 0 & \text{if } s_i < 0 \end{cases}$$

satisfies

$$\text{sign}\left(\sum_{i=1}^{n} w_i x_i \right) = \text{sign}\left(\sum_{i=1}^{n} s_i x_i \right) \quad \forall x \in \Omega$$

It suffices to show that if

$$\sum_{i=1}^{n} s_i x_i > 0$$

then

$$\sum_{i=1}^{n} w_i x_i > 0$$

Assume to the contrary that

$$\sum_{i=1}^{n} s_i x_i > 0 \quad \text{and} \quad \sum_{i=1}^{n} w_i x_i \leq 0$$

Denote by G the set of indices for which $s_i < 0$. Then

$$\sum_{i=1}^{n} s_i x_i = \sum_{i=1}^{n} w_i x_i + \sum_{i \in G} s_i x_i$$

and by assumption

$$\sum_{i \in G} s_i x_i > 0$$

Note that some of the x_i, $i \in G$, equal -1 since $s_i < 0$ for all $i \in G$. Transform the original profile $x \in X(1)$ to a new profile x'

$$x' = \begin{cases} x_i & i \notin G \\ 1 & i \in G \end{cases}$$

By the monotonicity of f, $x' \in X(1, f)$, and, in turn,

$$\sum_{i=1}^{n} s_i x_i' > 0$$

Again

$$\sum_{i=1}^{n} s_i x_i' = \sum_{i=1}^{n} w_i x_i' + \sum_{i \in G} s_i x_i'$$

However, now

$$\sum_{i=1}^{n} w_i x_i' = \sum_{i=1}^{n} w_i x_i \leq 0$$

and

$$\sum_{i \in G} s_i x_i' = \sum_{i \in G} s_i < 0$$

which implies that

$$\sum_{i=1}^{n} s_i x_i' < 0$$

A contradiction. The semi-positive vector w can be readily transformed to a semi-positive integral vector w' (by rational approximation followed by multiplication in a common denominator as in note 5) satisfying

$$\text{sign}\left(\sum_{i=1}^{n} w_i' x_i\right) = \text{sign}\left(\sum_{i=1}^{n} w_i x_i\right) = f$$

Theorem 2.4.2 Let $n \leqslant 5$. Then a DDR f is a DWMR iff it is monotonic and neutral.

Proof: Let $D(x) = |\{i \mid x_i = 1\}|$ and $D^l = \{x \in \Omega \mid D(x) = l\}$, $l = 0, \ldots, n$. Clearly

$$\bigcup_{l=0}^{n} D^l = \Omega$$

Consider the set D^{n-1}. Then for any DDR f there are three possibilities:

(1) $f(x^1) = -1$ for a single profile $x^1 \in D^{n-1}$, i.e. $x^1 = (x_1^1, \ldots, x_n^1)$ and

$$x_i^1 = \begin{cases} 1 & i \neq r \\ -1 & i = r \end{cases}$$

$$f(x) = 1 \forall x \in \{D^{n-1} \setminus x^1\}$$

(2) $f(x) = 1 \forall x \in D^{n-1}$

(3) $f(x^1) = f(x^2) = -1$ for at least two distinct profiles $x^1, x^2 \in D^{n-1}$.

The following two lemmas deal with possibilities (1) and (3) respectively.

Lemma 1 Suppose f is monotonic and neutral. If possibility (1) holds true, then $f(x) = x_r$.

Proof: By assumption, $f(x^1) = -1 = x_r$
By neutrality, $f(-x^1) = 1 = x_r$
By monotonicity, $f(x) = x_r, \forall x \in \Omega$

Lemma 2 Suppose f is monotonic and neutral. Then (3) is impossible.

Proof: Suppose to the contrary, that there exist $x^1, x^2 \in D^{n-1}$, $x^1 \neq x^2$ and $f(x^1) = f(x^2) = -1$. Note that $-x^1 \leqslant x^2$. By neutrality $f(-x^1) = 1$, which is in contradiction to the monotonicity.

We now proceed with the main proof. For $n < 3$ the proof is trivial.

(i) Let $n = 3$. By unanimity (see note 6), $f(x) = 1$ $\forall x \in D^3$ and $f(x) = -1$ $\forall x \in D^0$. Consider the set D^2.

Case 1: If possibility (1) holds true, then by Lemma 1, $f(x) = \text{sign } (w \cdot x)$[8] where w might be any permutation of $(1, 0, 0)$.

Case 2: If possibility (2) holds true, then $f(x) = 1$ $\forall x \in D^2$, and by neutrality, $f(x) = -1$ $\forall x \in D^1$. We thus get $f(x) = \text{sign } (w \cdot x)$ where $w = (1, 1, 1)$.

(ii) Let $n = 4$. By unanimity, $f(x) = 1$ $\forall x \in D^4$ and $f(x) = -1$ $\forall x \in D^0$. Consider the set D^3.

Case 1: If possibility (1) holds true, then by Lemma 1, $f(x) = \text{sign } (w \cdot x)$ where w might be any permutation of $(1, 0, 0, 0)$. If possibility (2) holds true, then $f(x) = 1$ $\forall x \in D^3$, and by neutrality, $f(x) = -1$ $\forall x \in D^1$. Consider the remaining set D^2.

Case 2: With no loss of generality, take any three out of the $\binom{4}{2} = 6$ voting profiles in D^2 and let

$$f(x) = 1 \; \forall x \in \{(1, 1, -1, -1), (1, -1, 1, -1), (1, -1, -1, 1)\}$$

By neutrality,

$$f(x) = -1 \; \forall x \in \{(-1, -1, 1, 1), (-1, 1, -1, 1), (-1, 1, 1, -1)\}$$

In this case $f(x) = \text{sign } (w \cdot x)$ where $w = (2, 1, 1, 1)$. By symmetry, there exist four possibilities such that $f(x) = \text{sign} (w \cdot x)$ where w is any permutation of $(2, 1, 1, 1)$.

Case 3: Now let

$$f(x) = 1 \; \forall x \in \{(-1, -1, 1, 1), (-1, 1, -1, 1), (-1, 1, 1, -1)\}$$

By neutrality,

$$f(x) = -1 \; \forall x \in \{(1, 1, -1, -1), (1, -1, 1, -1), (1, -1, -1, 1)\}$$

In this case, $f(x) = \text{sign } (w \cdot x)$ where $w = (0, 1, 1, 1)$. By symmetry, there exist four possibilities such that $f(x) = \text{sign } (w \cdot x)$ where w is any permutation of $(0, 1, 1, 1)$. Note that in general there exist 2^6 possible different forms for the restriction of f on D^2. By neutrality there exist only 2^3 such forms and therefore cases (2) and (3) are exhaustive.

(iii) Let $n = 5$. Utilizing Lemmas 1 and 2 we can verify that there are seven possible cases.[9] Specifically, $f(x) = \text{sign } (w \cdot x)$, where w is a permutation of one of the following set of weights $(1, 0, 0, 0, 0), (1, 1, 1, 0, 0), (2, 1, 1, 1, 0), (3, 1, 1, 1, 1), (1, 1, 1, 1, 1), (2, 2, 1, 1, 1), (3, 2, 2, 1, 1)$.

Theorem 2.5.1 For $n \leqslant 5$, $W(n) = E(n)$.

Proof: The proof is based on Theorem 2.4.2 and the following lemma.

Lemma 3 If a DDR f' is non-monotonic, then f' is inefficient.

Proof: If f' is non-monotonic, then there must exist two voting profiles x^1 and x^2 such that $x^1 \geqslant x^2$ and $f'(x^1) < f'(x^2)$, or $f'(x^1) = -1$ and $f'(x^2) = 1$. Define

$$f(x) = \begin{cases} 1 & x = x^1 \\ f'(x) & \text{otherwise} \end{cases} \quad \text{and} \quad \bar{f}(x) = \begin{cases} -1 & x = x^2 \\ f'(x) & \text{otherwise} \end{cases}$$

If a is the correct alternative, then $\pi(f, p) \geqslant \pi(f, p)$ for all pf with strict inequality for all $p \in P' = \{p \mid 1 \geqslant p_i > \frac{1}{2}\}$. If b is the correct alternative, then $\pi(\bar{f}, p) \geqslant \pi(f', p)$ for all $p \in P$ with strict inequality for all $p \in P'$.

Lemma 1 and Theorem 2.4.2 directly imply that a rule is a DWMR iff it is efficient.

Theorem 2.5.2 A DWMR f is efficient relative to p^0 if $w_i > w_j$ whenever $p_i^0 > p_j^0$.

Proof: With no loss of generality suppose that $p_1^0 > p_2^0$ and $w_1 < w_2$. Denote by w' the permutation on w that interchanges w_1 and w_2 only, i.e. $w' = (w_2, w_1, w_3, \ldots, w_n)$. We will show that $\pi(f(x; w'), p) > \pi(f(x; w), p)$ $\forall p \in G(p^0)$.

Partition the set Ω into the following three subsets

$$\Omega_0 = \{(y_1, \ldots, y_n) \mid y_1 = y_2, \ y_i \in \{1, -1\}, \ \forall i \in N\}$$
$$\Omega_1 = \{(y_1, \ldots, y_n) \mid y_1 = 1, \ y_2 = -1, \ y_i \in \{1, -1\}, \ \forall i = 3, \ldots, n\}$$
$$\Omega_2 = \{(y_1, \ldots, y_n) \mid y_1 = -1, \ y_2 = 1, \ y_i \in \{1, -1\}, \ \forall i \in 3, \ldots, n)$$

Denote by Ω_z the set of 2^{n-2} possible restricted random variables $z = (y_3, \ldots, y_n)$. For a given $z \in \Omega_z$ partition the set of indices $\{3, \ldots, n\}$ into A_z and B_z such that $i \in A_z$ if $x_i = 1$ and $i \in B_z$ if $x_i = -1$. Note that $f(y; w) = f(y; w')$ $\forall y \in \Omega^0$. Hence,

$$\sum_{y \in \Omega} g(y)[f(y; w') - f(y; w)] = \sum_{z \in \Omega} p_1(1 - p_2)KL - \sum_{z \in \Omega_z} p_1(1 - p_2)KM$$

$$+ \sum_{z \in \Omega_z} (1 - p_1)p_2 KM - \sum_{z \in \Omega_z} (1 - p_1)p_2 KL$$

$$= \sum_{z \in \Omega_z} [p_1(1 - p_2) - p_2(1 - p_1)]K(L - M) > 0$$

where

$$K = \sum_{i \in A_z} p_i \prod_{j \in B_z} (1 - p_j)$$

$$L = \text{sign}\left[w_2 - w_1 + \sum_{i \in A_z} w_i - \sum_{j \in B_z} w_j \right]$$

$$M = \text{sign}\left[w_1 - w_2 + \sum_{i \in A_z} w_i - \sum_{j \in B_z} w_j \right]$$

and $L - M > 0$, since $w_2 > w_1$.
By neutrality,

$$\sum_{y \in \Omega} g(y) f(y; w') = 2\pi(f(x; w'), p) - 1$$

and

$$\sum_{y \in \Omega} g(y) f(y; w') = 2\pi(f(x; w), p) - 1$$

so that

$$\sum_{y \in \Omega} g(y) [f(y; w') - f(y; w)] > 0$$

$$\Rightarrow \pi(f(x; w'), p) > \pi(f(x; w), p) \quad \forall p \in G(p^0)$$

CHAPTER 3

Costs of decision rules

3.1   Introduction

In the preceding chapter the probability of the group choosing correctly, denoted by π, is posed as the sole target in choosing among the feasible decision rules. Given the skill of the group members, the optimal rule is identified and some of its properties are discussed. Confining the discussion to only two symmetric alternatives and assuming that there exists no conflict of interest among the group members, the optimal rule turns out to be a Pareto efficient rule as well as a solution to the problem of maximizing the group expected common utility.

A serious drawback of the basic uncertain dichotomous choice model is its total disregard of the cost element associated with the utilization of different decision rules.[1] This chapter relaxes the assumption that the costs associated with any decision rule f are identically equal to zero and focuses on the implications of extending the basic model to account for decision-making costs. Instead of maximizing $\pi(f, p)$ with respect to neutral decision rules f for any given vector of skills p, this chapter is concerned with the maximization of group expected benefit $B\pi(f, p) - C(f, p)$ with respect to feasible rules f. As in Section 2.2, $B = B_s - B_f > 0$ is the net benefit of a correct decision. Obviously, the basic problem is a special case of this whenever $C(f, p)$ is identically equal to zero. Note that under the more general problem the decision rule that maximizes the group expected net income is not necessarily Pareto efficient unless the common utility of the group members is linear. In other words, if the group welfare indicator is linear then the objective of maximizing expected net benefit is equivalent to the maximization of the group expected welfare.

The cost function $C(f, p)$ may consist of several elements and the weights of these may certainly vary according to decisional circumstances. $C(f, p)$ comprises direct costs of using and operating the decision rule itself as well as indirect costs such as consulting fees charged by experts. Such fees may or may not depend on the expertise levels of the individuals needed for the operation of f. Some cost factors are obviously pecuniary, but some might be shadow prices which reflect opportunity losses. For instance, under emergency circumstances, when there is a severe shortage of time, certain rules are associated with extremely high alternative costs. In cases where certain decision rules are subject to legal regulations or in cases where some institutional restrictions are externally imposed on the use of certain decision rules, the cost attached to these rules might become prohibitively high.

In short, a model that focuses on the probability of obtaining a correct decision is certainly limited as it ignores crucial economic aspects: the net benefit associated with a correct choice B and the costs associated with the utilization of decision rules $C(f, p)$.

The structure of this chapter is as follows: Section 3.2 deals with experts possessing identical levels of decisional skills. Under such circumstances decision-making costs depend merely on the size of the decision-making body. Since homogeneity of decisional skills implies the superiority of simple majority rule the general problem reduces to the problem of determining the optimal size of the group. Section 3.3 relaxes this assumption and presents some implications for the case of heterogeneous skills. Section 3.4 focuses on the special case where the cost associated with one or more of the decision rules is prohibitively high. Here, the problem is to find the second or the third best solution. Section 3.5 analyzes another special case where the decisional skills are subject to potential variability. Here the cost associated with a decision rule is also a function of the sensitivity of the rule to such potential variability of skills. The optimal rule even with respect to the simple objective of maximizing π is not necessarily the most robust one so the problem in such a case is to consider the trade-off between the likelihood of correct decision and the immunity of the rule with respect to uncertain skill variability.

3.2   The optimal size of a homogeneous decision-making body

By Corollary 2.3.1 (3), the existence of identical skills is a sufficient condition for the superiority of simple majority rules. Therefore the set of potentially optimal rules comprises simple majority rules only. In turn, there is a one-to-one correspondence between each of these rules and the number of participants actually required in the decision-making process. So the cost of utilizing rules is just a function of the size of the decision group and the problem of maximizing $B\pi - C$ with respect to f is reduced in the case of equally skilled individuals to the problem of maximizing $B\pi - C$ with respect to the size of the decision group. More specifically, consider first an unlimited number of experts with a homogeneous decisional skill p. The optimal decision rule in this case is a simple majority rule (assume, with some loss of generality, that the number of experts actually participating in the voting process is always odd, i.e. $m = 2k + 1$ where k is an integer). The probability of the group making a correct decision using simple majority rule is

$$(3.2.1) \quad \pi(p,k) = \sum_{i=k+1}^{2k+1} \binom{2k+1}{i} p^i (1-p)^{2k+1-i}$$

In the absence of cost it is always worthwhile to exhaust the number of experts n available in order to maximize π because for $p > \frac{1}{2}$

$$d\pi(p,k)/dk = \pi(p, k+1) - \pi(p, k)$$
$$= \binom{2k+1}{k+1} p^{k+1}(1-p)^{k+1}(2p-1) > 0$$

and

$$\lim_{k \to \infty} \pi(p, k) = 1$$

In other words, it is inefficient to assign zero weight to some of the available experts. In fact, this result is attributed to Condorcet (1785).[2]

In reality using experts is not a costless activity. Assume that the cost function $C(p, 2k+1)$ satisfies $dC/dk = C(p, 2k+3) - C(p, 2k+1) \geqslant 0$, $dC/dp \geqslant 0$, and $d^2C/dk^2 = d(dC/dk)/dk \geqslant 0$. That is, the cost function is strictly increasing in size of the group N and increasing in decisional skills p and the marginal cost of group size increases in k. For instance, let $C(p, 2k+1) = (k + \frac{1}{2})c(p)$ where $c(p)/2$ is the constant marginal cost of using an expert. Since

$$d^2\pi/dk^2 = d\pi/dk[4p(1-p)$$
$$- 1 - 2p(1-p)/(k+2)] < 0$$

and, by assumption, $d^2C/dk^2 \geqslant 0$ there always exists a unique solution k^* to the problem

$$(3.2.2) \quad \max_k [B\pi(p, 2k+1) - C(p, 2k+1)]$$

Ignoring indivisibilities, the solution k^* equates marginal cost and marginal benefit or, more specifically, k^* fulfils $Bd\pi/dk \geqslant dC/dk$ for all k such that $k \leqslant k^*$ and $Bd\pi/dk \leqslant dC/dk$ for all k such that $k \geqslant k^*$. Moreover, it is easy to verify that $dk^*/dB \geqslant 0$.

To illustrate the significance of incorporating costs into the objective function consider the following special case where $B = 1$, $p = 0.8$ and $C(0.8, 2k+1) = 0.03k$. In this case,

n	k	$\pi(0.8,\ 2k+1)$	$B\pi - C$
1	0	0.800	0.800
3	1	0.896	0.806
5	2	0.946	0.796

We see that although the use of five experts instead of three increases the probability of a correct decision from 0.896 to 0.946, the total expected net benefit $B\pi - C$ decreases from 0.806 to 0.796 because of the increasing cost. Since the cost is linear in k and the benefit $B\pi$ is concave in k any additional increase in k would further reduce the total expected net benefit so that the optimal group size is $n^* = 3$ or $k^* = 1$.

3.3   Heterogeneous skills

We now turn to the more general case where the experts' decisional skills are not necessarily identical. Introducing the cost element $C(f, p)$ into the basic model modifies problem (2.2.1) to the more general form

$$(3.3.1) \quad \max_{f \in M} [B\pi(f, p) - C(f, p)]$$

As before $\pi(f, p)$ is the probability of the group making a correct choice applying the decision rule f. Here p is the skill vector $p = (p_1, \ldots, p_n)$. In this more general case the extension of problem (3.2.2) to (3.3.1) complicates matters in two crucial respects. First, π cannot be simply expressed as in the previous case of homogeneous decisional skills (see (3.2.1)). Second, the cost function no longer depends merely on the size of the group N. It should be noted that in the heterogeneous case the significance of the group size is further reduced because $d\pi/dn$ is not necessarily positive any more and the probability π does not necessarily tend to infinity with the number of experts even if all the values of p_i are larger than $\frac{1}{2}$. To see this point, let $\beta_i = \ln p_i/(1 - p_i)$ as in the previous chapter. By Corollary 2.3.1 (2) the expert rule is optimal if and only if

$$\beta_1 > \sum_{i=2}^{n} \beta_i$$

and in such a case $\pi = p_1$. Let

$$\lambda_j = \beta_1 / \sum_{i=2}^{j} \beta_i > 1$$

and suppose that $\frac{1}{2} < p_{j+1} < 1/[1 + \exp(-\lambda_j)]$, so that $0 < \beta_{j+1} < \lambda_j$. It is easy to verify that in this case

$$\beta_1 > \sum_{j=2}^{m} \beta_j$$

for every m. So that $d\pi/dn = 0$ and

$$\lim_{n \to \infty} \pi = p_1 < 1$$

even if all the values of p_i are larger than $\frac{1}{2}$. However, if there exists some $\varepsilon > 0$ such that all the values of p_i are larger than $\frac{1}{2} + \varepsilon$, then

$$\lim_{n \to \infty} \pi = 1$$

In this case, for every n, $\pi(p, f) > \pi(q, f)$ where q is an n-tuple all of whose components are equal to $\frac{1}{2} + \varepsilon$, since

$$\lim_{n \to \infty} \pi(q, f) = 1$$

we also obtain that

$$\lim_{n \to \infty} \pi(p, f) = 1$$

In the remainder of this section we present two examples that illustrate the significance of the extended model and clarify some of its major economic implications for the consulting industry.

Consider a government agency facing the execution of a project that belongs to the all-or-nothing type that can either succeed or fail. The agency has to choose one of two available methods of handling the project, and to improve the chances of making the correct decision it can employ the consulting services of four firms numbered one through four. These firms are represented by the vector of skills $(p_1, p_2, p_3, p_4) = (0.9, 0.9, 0.8, 0.7)$, where p_i is the probability that firm i recommends the correct decision. By Table 2.1, for $n = 4$ there are three reasonable weighted majority rules. The expert rule (f_1); the restricted simple majority rule, or simple majority rule applied among the three most competent experts (f_2); and simple majority rule with a tie-breaking chairman (f_3) (the most qualified expert being the chairman). The vectors of weights defining these three possible relevant rules are $(1, 0, 0, 0)$, $(1, 1, 1, 0)$ and $(2, 1, 1, 1)$ respectively. The respective probabilities of selecting the correct alternative corresponding to these rules are denoted by π_1, π_2, and π_3. Direct calculation shows that, with the skill vector in our example, $\pi_2 > \pi_3 > \pi_1$, i.e. the largest probability that the agency will make the correct decision is obtained when applying the restricted simple majority rule. In other words, the agency hires the three most competent firms and a final decision is made by applying the simple majority rule.

At this stage assume that:

(a) The government agency operates as a private firm trying to maximize its expected benefit.

(b) Successful completion of the project will yield a net benefit (total revenue minus total costs, excluding consulting costs) of B_s. In the case of failure, the net benefit equals $B_f < B_s$. The two available alternatives are symmetric in the sense that $B_s(B_f)$ is independent of the particular alternative correctly (mistakenly) chosen.

(c) The price of the consulting service offered by firm i is equal to c_i. Let us initially assume a uniform consulting price, i.e. $(c_1, c_2, c_3, c_4) = (1, 1, 1, 1)$. The consulting costs associated with any decision procedure f are denoted by $C(f)$. By assumption, the agency's aim is to select that relevant weighted majority rule that maximizes expected benefit,[3] i.e.

$$\max_{f \in \{f_1, f_2, f_3\}} \{\pi(f, p)B_s + [1 - \pi(f, p)]B_f - C(f)\}$$

or equivalently

$$\max_{f \in \{f_1, f_2, f_3\}} \{\pi(f, p)B - C(f)\}$$

where $B = B_s - B_f$. In our particular case, $\pi(f_2, p) > \pi(f_3, p)$ and $C(f_2) < C(f_3)$, so that f_3 (simple majority rule with a tie-breaking chairman) is inferior to f_2 (the restricted simple majority rule) for any value of B (the difference between success and failure in terms of the project's net benefit). The real choice is, therefore, between f_1, the expert rule, and f_2 the restricted simple majority rule. Let $\Delta \pi_{21} = \pi_2 - \pi_1$ and $\Delta C_{21} = C(f_2) - C(f_1)$, so that f_2 is the optimal procedure whenever $(\Delta \pi_{21} B - \Delta C_{21}) > 0$, f_1 is optimal if the inequality is reversed, and the two rules are equivalent if $(\Delta \pi_{21} B - \Delta C_{21}) = 0$. This optimal criterion is valid for any vector of skills (p_1, p_2, p_3, p_4) and cost vector (c_1, c_2, c_3, c_4) satisfying $p_1 = p_2, p_3 \neq p_4$ and $c_1 \leqslant c_2 \leqslant c_3 \leqslant c_4$.

A common tender system suggests the selection of the most highly qualified and least expensive candidate, if one exists, or if not, then selection of the candidate that is most satisfactory in terms of a combination of price and quality. We have shown that such a method might be less efficient than one that properly uses the combined consulting services of several candidates. In the above example, a sufficiently large difference in the net benefit of the project when comparing success to failure justifies a more intensive use of consulting services. More precisely, if $\Delta \pi_{21} B - \Delta C_{21} = 0.53B - 2 > 0$, i.e. if $B > 37.73$, then three consulting firms (firm 1, firm 2 and firm 3) should be hired rather than the single consulting firm (firm 1) that is the most highly skilled and least expensive. When $B = 37.73$, f_1 and f_2 are equivalent.

Usually, however, consulting prices are not inversely related to quality. The government agency might therefore need to consider all weighted majority rules, not necessarily the relevant ones alone. When four consulting firms are available, there are twelve such rules ($f_1, \ldots, f_{12}$): four restricted simple majority rules; four simple majority rules with a tie-breaking chairman; and four single expert rules. The optimal rule f_j must now satisfy the condition

$$\Delta \pi_{ji} B - \Delta C_{ji} \geq 0 \quad \text{for every } i = 1, \ldots, 12$$

Application of the model to the consulting context seems to suggest an interesting explanation regarding the structural form of the consulting industry. One can hardly imagine two cinemas located in the same neighborhood such that one of the two always displays better movies for a lower price, or two gasoline stations where one is offering a better service as well as a lower price per gallon. It is quite obvious that sooner or later the less efficient firm has to shut down. On the other hand, it is quite possible to observe physicians operating in the same town and some of the less qualified among them stay in business, although they are charging higher fees for the same service offered by some of their superior colleagues. To illustrate this point we present the following simple numerical example. Consider three doctors with a skill vector equal to $(0.82, 0.80, 0.78)$ and a corresponding vector of consulting fees equal to $(2, 1, 6)$. Note that the least qualified doctor charges a rate which is three times higher than that of the most qualified one, and six times higher than the fee charged by expert 2, the second most qualified. By simple calculation it can be verified that if the net benefit of correct decision B is less than 1.25, no consulting is undertaken, if $1.25 < B < 2.44$, then the second most qualified doctor, who charges the lowest fee, will be taken as the only consultant, if $2.44 < B < 7.81$ the most qualified doctor will be used as the only advisor but for any value of B such that $7.81 < B$ even the least qualified and the most expensive doctor will be included in the decision group and a decision will be taken by simple majority rule. The probability of a correct decision in the last case is 0.896 which is larger than

$$0.82 = \max_i p_i$$

3.4 Ranking of rules

Suppose that a certain rule is institutionally prohibited. Within our model we can introduce such a constraint through a sufficient increase in the costs associated with the prohibited rule. In order to solve problem (3.3.1) for any given net benefit B, cost function C, and vector of decisional skills p, it is essential to identify all weighted majority rules for any given group of size n and to rank these rules by π. This section offers a simple ranking algorithm for the case $n = 4$ where, by Table 2.1, three weighted majority rules are relevant: f_1 with the vector of weights $(1, 0, 0, 0)$ and probability π_1, f_2 with the suitable vector $(1, 1, 1, 0)$ and the corresponding probability π_2 and f_3 defined by the vector $(2, 1, 1, 1)$ and yielding the probability π_3.

The necessary and sufficient conditions for the possible ranking of the three relevant rules in four-member panels of experts are given below.

Proposition 3.4.1 Let $n = 4$ and denote by α_i the odds of individual i making an incorrect decision; that is $\alpha_i = (1 - p_i)/p_i$.

If $\alpha_1 < \alpha_2\alpha_3\alpha_4$,	then $\pi_1 > \pi_3 > \pi_2$.
If $\alpha_1\alpha_4 > \alpha_2\alpha_3$,	then $\pi_2 > \pi_3 > \pi_1$.
If $\alpha_2\alpha_3 > \alpha_1 > \alpha_2\alpha_3\alpha_4$,	then $\pi_3 > \pi_1 > \pi_2$.
If $\alpha_1 > \alpha_2\alpha_3 > \alpha_1\alpha_4$,	then $\pi_3 > \pi_2 > \pi_1$.

Proof:

$$\pi_1 = \pi(f_1, p) = p_1$$

$$\pi_2 = \pi(f_2, p) = (1 - p_1)p_2p_3 + (1 - (1 - p_2)(1 - p_3))$$

$$\pi_3 = \pi(f_3, p) = (1 - p_1)p_2p_3p_4$$
$$+ p_1(1 - (1 - p_2)(1 - p_3)(1 - p_4))$$

$$\pi_2 - \pi_1 = p_1p_2p_3(\alpha_1 - \alpha_2\alpha_3)$$

$$\pi_3 - \pi_1 = p_1p_2p_3p_4(\alpha_1 - \alpha_2\alpha_3\alpha_4)$$

$$\pi_2 - \pi_3 = p_1p_2p_3p_4(\alpha_1\alpha_4 - \alpha_2\alpha_3)$$

The four assertions follow directly from these equations, since $\frac{1}{2} \leq p_i < 1$ and, hence, $0 < \alpha_i \leq 1$. The four conditions that appear in this proposition are exhaustive; therefore, they are the necessary and sufficient conditions for the possible rankings of the three rules.

The following four corollaries are directly obtained from Proposition 3.4.1.

Corollary 3.4.1 (1) In a three-member panel of experts, simple majority rule is superior to the expert rule if and only if $\alpha_1 > \alpha_2\alpha_3$.

Corollary 3.4.1 (2) In a three-member panel of experts, equality of skills between the two most competent experts is a sufficient condition for the superiority of simple majority rule over the expert rule.

Corollary 3.4.1 (3) In a four-member panel of experts, equality of skills between the two most competent experts implies that the restricted simple majority rule is superior to simple majority rule with a tie-breaking chairman, which is superior, in turn, to the expert rule. In short, $p_1 = p_2$ and $p_3 \neq p_4$ imply that $\pi_2 > \pi_3$.

Corollary 3.4.1 (4) In a four-member panel of experts, equality of skills between the two least competent experts implies that simple majority rule with a tie-breaking chairman is superior to the restricted simple majority rule. In short, $p_3 = p_4$ and $p_1 \neq p_2$ imply that $\pi_3 > \pi_2$.

Corollary 3.4.1 (1) provides us with a simple algorithm to find the optimal rule.[4] A simple example illustrating the use of this corollary is presented below.

A firm is divided into three major departments – production, marketing and personnel – and its board consists of the three department heads. Suppose that they have to select one and only one of the following restricted decision-making processes: (1) every problem would be decided upon by the relevant department head, (2) every problem would be decided upon by simple majority rule.

Suppose that each department head has a probability p to decide correctly on problems relevant to his department and a probability g ($\frac{1}{2} < g < p$) to decide correctly on issues involving his colleagues' departments.

Using the inequality in Corollary 3.4.1 (1) we can verify that the simple majority decision process is optimal if and only if g is such that

$$p > g > \frac{\sqrt{[p(1-p)]}}{1 + \sqrt{[p(1-p)]}}$$

For instance if p is equal to 0.8 or 0.9, then $\sqrt{[p(1-p)]}/(1 + \sqrt{[p(1-p)]})$ is equal to 2/3 and 3/4 respectively. Hence, whenever $4/5 > g > 2/3$ or $9/10 > g > 3/4$ respectively, the simple majority rule process is the better choice.

3.5 Potential variability of decisional skills

This section is concerned with a particular type of indirect costs associated with potential variability of the decision makers' skills.

In an uncertain environment decisional skills may decline due to the occurrence of different undesirable events. For example, consider the effect of bad weather, health or personal problems, industrial sabotage or absenteeism on individual decisional skills. Suppose that the potential for such variability of decisional skills can be represented by a single parameter denoted α. In many cases α can be interpreted as the probability of the occurrence of undesirable events. Let $\alpha = 0$ indicate a situation with no potential for skills variability.

The corresponding decline in the performance of the group (in terms of the particular objective function assumed for the group) while using the rule f, defines the costs associated with f. In other words, the costs $C(f)$ are naturally defined by the sensitivity of the rule to potential variability of skills. That is, $C(f, p, \alpha) = V(f, p, 0) - V(f, p, \alpha)$ where the objective function V depends on the rule employed by the group f on decisional skills of the individuals comprising the group $p = (p_1, \ldots, p_n)$ and on the parameter representing the potential for skills variability α.

Incorporating the parameter α into the model raises three interesting questions. First, how sensitive are different rules to potential variability of skills. Second, how does the relative sensitivity of different rules respond to variations in the parameter α. Third, what is the effect of potential decline in skills on the optimal rule for the group. Put differently, what is the optimal rule given the potential skills variability and can this rule differ from the optimal rule when $\alpha = 0$.

These three questions are analyzed and resolved for the case of three-member groups assuming three particular patterns of potential decline in individual skills. Specifically, we analyze the case where each individual skill may totally vanish when some undesirable state of nature materializes. The probability of occurrence of such a state is assumed to be equal to α. In this case we provide the complete answers to the optimality and sensitivity issues mentioned above. Then alternative models are proposed assuming, again, panels of experts consisting of three members. Here the potential of skills variability is studied using a stylized model of decisional sabotage. Specifically, we assume that the group might be subjected to the injurious activities of each (or, alternatively, a single) decision maker in probability α where the saboteur will do his best to reduce the performance of the group. We also discuss the particular case of complete ignorance regarding eventual individual decisional skills. Partial answers to the optimality and sensitivity issues are provided.

3.5.1 *Loss of decisional competence*

Consider three individuals, 1, 2, 3, confronting two mutually exclusive and symmetric alternatives and sharing a common system of norms. Let $(p_1, p_2, p_3) = p$ denote the skill vector. Now suppose that each individual decisional skill may totally vanish with probability α. That is, for each decision maker there exists some state of nature that results in the decline of his competence level from p_i to $\frac{1}{2}$. That state of nature occurs in probability α. For simplicity we assume that all three individuals are equally vulnerable to such skill depreciation, that is the same value of α applies to all group members. The potential for loss of skills may differently affect the two relevant decision rules. Denoting by $C(f)$ the costs associated with potential skills dissipation for rule f and assuming, again, a linear objective function our problem becomes

$$(3.5.1) \quad \max_{f \in \{e, m\}} V(f, p, \alpha) = [B\pi(f, p) - C(f, p, \alpha)]$$

where e and m denote the expert and the majority rules respectively. In general,

Table 3.1

(1) p	(2) $\Pr(p)$	(3) $\pi(e, p)$	(4) $\pi(m, p)$
p_1, p_2, p_3	$(1-\alpha)^3$	p_1	$p_1p_2p_3 + p_1p_2(1-p_3) + p_1(1-p_2)p_3 + (1-p_1)p_2p_3$
$p_1, p_2, \frac{1}{2}$	$(1-\alpha)^2\alpha$	p_1	$\frac{1}{2}[2p_1p_2 + p_1(1-p_2) + (1-p_1)p_2] = \frac{1}{2}[p_1+p_2]$
$p_1, \frac{1}{2}, p_3$	$(1-\alpha)^2\alpha$	p_1	$\frac{1}{2}[2p_1p_3 + p_1(1-p_3) + (1-p_1)p_3] = \frac{1}{2}[p_1+p_3]$
$\frac{1}{2}, p_2, p_3$	$(1-\alpha)^2\alpha$	$\frac{1}{2}$	$\frac{1}{2}[2p_2p_3 + p_2(1-p_3) + (1-p_2)p_3] = \frac{1}{2}[p_2+p_3]$
$p_1, \frac{1}{2}, \frac{1}{2}$	$(1-\alpha)\alpha^2$	p_1	$\frac{1}{4}[3p_1 + (1-p_1)]$
$\frac{1}{2}, p_2, \frac{1}{2}$	$(1-\alpha)\alpha^2$	$\frac{1}{2}$	$\frac{1}{4}[3p_2 + (1-p_2)]$
$\frac{1}{2}, \frac{1}{2}, p_3$	$(1-\alpha)\alpha^2$	$\frac{1}{2}$	$\frac{1}{4}[3p_3 + (1-p_3)]$
$\frac{1}{2}, \frac{1}{2}, \frac{1}{2}$	α^3	$\frac{1}{2}$	$\frac{1}{2}$

$C(f, p, \alpha) = C(s_\alpha^f)$ where $s_\alpha^f = \pi(f, p, 0) - \pi(f, p, \alpha)$ is a measure of sensitivity. That is, the costs depend on the sensitivity measure s_α^f. For simplicity assume the particular form $C(s_\alpha^f) = Bs_\alpha^f$. Therefore in this special case of indirect cost the general problem (3.5.1) is reduced to

$$(3.5.2) \quad \max_{f \in \{e, m\}} B\pi(f, p, \alpha)$$

Having incorporated the potential for skills variability into the standard dichotomous choice model we now turn to the analysis of the sensitivity measures s_α^e and s_α^m and to the study of the effect of potential competence depreciation on the optimal decision rule for the group.

Column (1) in Table 3.1 specifies the eight skill configurations possible under the special case of total loss of skills. The corresponding probabilities of occurrence for the possible vectors of skills appear in column (2). The corresponding values of $\pi(e, p)$ and $\pi(m, p)$ are contained in columns (3) and (4). For example, the probability that there is no decline in individual decisional skills is $(1 - \alpha)^3$ and in such a case the probability that the group makes a correct choice using the expert rule is $\pi(e, p) = \pi_0^e = p_1$. The collective probability of choosing correctly using the simple majority rule is

$$\pi(m, p) = \pi_0^m = p_1p_2p_3 + (1 - p_1)p_2p_3 + p_1(1 - p_2)p_3 + p_1p_2(1 - p_3)$$

With Table 3.1 the group probability of making the correct judgement can directly be computed using the two alternative rules and taking account of the potential for skills depreciation. Specifically we obtain

$$\pi(e, p, \alpha) = \pi_\alpha^e = (1 - \alpha)\pi_0^e + \frac{\alpha}{2} < \pi_0^e$$

$$\pi(m, p, \alpha) = \pi_\alpha^m = (1 - \alpha)^3 \pi_0^m + \alpha(1 - \alpha)\left(1 - \frac{\alpha}{2}\right)(p_1 + p_2 + p_3)$$

$$+ \alpha^2(1 - \alpha)\frac{3}{4} + \frac{\alpha^3}{2} < \pi_0^m$$

Recall that the sensitivity of the two rules to the parameter α is given by $s_\alpha^e = \pi_0^e - \pi_\alpha^e$ and $s_\alpha^m = \pi_0^m - \pi_\alpha^m$. The sign of $(s_\alpha^e - s_\alpha^m)$ determines the relative sensitivity of the two rules for a given value of the parameter α. The sign of the derivative $d(s_\alpha^e - s_\alpha^m)/d\alpha$ indicates how the relative sensitivity changes with α. Finally, the sign of $(\pi_\alpha^e - \pi_\alpha^m)$ determines, for a given α, which of the two rules is the better one.

The following theorem provides the necessary and sufficient conditions for the determination of the signs of the above terms.

Proposition 3.5.1 Let $\delta = \pi_0^m - \pi_0^e$ and $\beta = (p_3 - \frac{1}{2}) - (p_1 - p_2)$.

(1) If $\delta \geq 0$, then $\forall \alpha$, $\pi_\alpha^m - \pi_\alpha^e > 0$, $s_\alpha^e - s_\alpha^m > 0$ and $d(s_\alpha^e - s_\alpha^m)/d\alpha > 0$.
(2) If $\delta < 0$, and $\beta > 0$, then
    (a) $\forall \alpha$, $s_\alpha^e - s_\alpha^m > 0$ and $d(s_\alpha^e - s_\alpha^m)/d\alpha > 0$.
    (b) $\exists \alpha_0$ such that $\forall \alpha \neq \alpha_0$ $(\pi_\alpha^m - \pi_\alpha^e)(\alpha - \alpha_0) > 0$.
(3) If $\delta < 0$ and $\beta < 0$, then
    (a) $\forall \alpha$, $\pi_\alpha^m - \pi_\alpha^e < 0$.
    (b) $\forall \alpha$, $(s_\alpha^m - s_\alpha^e)(\beta - \delta) > 0$ and $(\beta - \delta)d(s_\alpha^e - s_\alpha^m)/d\alpha > 0$, assuming $\beta \neq \delta$.

Proof: By direct calculations we can obtain

$$\pi_\alpha^m - \pi_\alpha^e = (1 - \alpha)^3 \delta + [(1 - \alpha)^3 - (1 - \alpha)]p_1$$

$$+ \alpha(1 - \alpha)\left(1 - \frac{\alpha}{2}\right)(p_1 + p_2 + p_3)$$

$$+ \frac{\alpha^3}{2} - \frac{\alpha}{2} + \frac{3}{4}\alpha^2(1 - \alpha)$$

$$= (1 - \alpha)^3 \delta + \alpha(1 - \alpha)\left(\frac{\alpha}{2} - 1\right)p_1$$

$$+ \alpha(1 - \alpha)\left(1 - \frac{\alpha}{2}\right)(p_2 + p_3 - \frac{1}{2})$$

$$= (1 - \alpha)^3 \delta + [1 - (1 - \alpha)^3][p_2 + p_3 - p_1 - \frac{1}{2}]$$

so that $\forall \alpha$

$$(3.5.3) \quad \pi_\alpha^m - \pi_\alpha^e = (1 - \alpha)^3 \delta + [1 - (1 - \alpha)^3]\beta$$

and by definition

(3.5.4) $\quad s_\alpha^e - s_\alpha^m = [1 - (1 - \alpha)^3](\beta - \delta)$

By assumption, $p_3 > \frac{1}{2}$. Therefore $2p_3(p_2 - \frac{1}{2}) > (p_2 - \frac{1}{2})$ or $2p_2p_3 > p_2 + p_3 - \frac{1}{2}$. Multiplying both sides of this later inequality by $1 - p_2 - p_3 < 0$ we get

$$2p_2p_3(1 - p_2 - p_3) < (p_2 + p_3 - \frac{1}{2})(1 - p_2 - p_3)$$

or

$$p_2p_3(2 - 2p_2 - 2p_3) = p_2p_3[(1 + \frac{1}{2} - p_2 - p_3) - (p_2 + p_3 - \frac{1}{2})]$$
$$< (p_2 + p_3 - \frac{1}{2})(1 - p_2 - p_3)$$

or

$$p_2p_3(1 + \frac{1}{2} - p_2 - p_3) < (p_2 + p_3 - \frac{1}{2})(1 - p_2 - p_3 + p_2p_3)$$
$$= (p_2 + p_3 - \frac{1}{2})(1 - p_2)(1 - p_3)$$

or

$$p_2p_3 < (p_2 + p_3 - \frac{1}{2})[p_2p_3 + (1 - p_2)(1 - p_3)]$$

or

(3.5.5) $\quad \delta < \beta[p_2p_3 + (1 - p_2)(1 - p_3)]$

The proof of the various claims can now be directly obtained from (3.5.3), (3.5.4) and (3.5.5).

Suppose $\delta \geqslant 0$. Then by (3.5.5) $\beta > \delta$ and by (3.5.3) $\beta > \pi_\alpha^m - \pi_\alpha^e > \delta > 0$. By (3.5.4), $s_\alpha^e - s_\alpha^m > 0$ and $d(s_\alpha^e - s_\alpha^m)/d\alpha > 0$. Which establishes (1). Suppose $\delta < 0$ and $\beta > 0$. Then by (3.5.3), $d(\pi_\alpha^m - \pi_\alpha^e)/d\alpha > 0$ and so there is α_0 for which $\pi_\alpha^m = \pi_\alpha^e$ or $(\pi_\alpha^m - \pi_\alpha^e)(\alpha - \alpha_0) > 0$ which establishes (2) (b). By (3.5.4), $s_\alpha^e - s_\alpha^m > 0$ and $d(s_\alpha^e - s_\alpha^m)/d\alpha > 0$ which establishes (2) (a). Suppose $\delta < 0$ and $\beta < 0$, then by (3.5.3), $\pi_\alpha^m - \pi_\alpha^e < 0$. By (3.5.4), for $\delta \neq \beta$, $(s_\alpha^e - s_\alpha^m)(\beta - \delta) > 0$ and $(\beta - \delta)d(s_\alpha^e - s_\alpha^m)/d\alpha > 0$ which establishes (3).

The above theorem states the necessary and sufficient conditions for the possible sensitivity and performance relationships of the two rules using the terms δ and β. Two important implications emerge. Except in the case where the difference $p_1 - p_2$ is very large (such that $\beta < \delta < 0$) the expert rule is more sensitive than the simple majority rule. Furthermore this difference in sensitivity increases with the probability α of skills decline. If, however, $\beta < \delta < 0$, for example $p_1 = 0.9$, $p_2 = p_3 = 0.6$ and so $\beta = -0.2$, and $\delta = -0.18$, then simple majority rule turns out to be the more sensitive rule. The second implication concerns the possibility of change in the optimal rule. If $\pi_0^m > \pi_0^e$, then $\pi_\alpha^m > \pi_\alpha^e$ for all α. That is, the superiority of simple majority rule is invariant to the introduction of potential loss of skills, regardless of its intensity. But if $\pi_0^m < \pi_0^e$, and $\beta > 0$, then there exists some α_0 such that for all

$\alpha > \alpha_0$, $\pi_\alpha^m > \pi_\alpha^e$. For example, let $p_2 = p_3 = 0.75$ and $p_1 = 0.9 + \gamma$ where $0 < \gamma < 0.1$. In this case $\beta = 0.1 - \gamma$ and

$$\alpha_0(\gamma) = 1 - \left(\frac{0.1 - \gamma}{0.1 - 0.375\gamma} \right)^{1/3}$$

and $d\alpha_0(\gamma)/d\gamma > 0$.

3.5.2 *Alternative special cases of skills variability*

A slight variation of the framework presented in the preceding section can be used to model decisional sabotage. Skills variability under such circumstances may represent the deliberate hostile activities of certain organizations (e.g. competing companies), and in any event the individual (s) involved, the saboteurs, act intentionally in a diametrically opposed way to the group objective. That is, the saboteur, if participating in the decision-making process, does his best to reduce the performance of the group. We present below two simple versions of the decisional sabotage model and briefly and partially illustrate their effect on the comparison between the expert rule and simple majority rule.

Decisional sabotage: Case 1

Suppose that each individual is a saboteur with probability α. If individual i is indeed a resolute saboteur his probability of choosing correctly is $(1 - p_i)$ rather than p_i. Constructing a table analogous to Table 3.1, using the notation of the previous section and employing similar straightforward algebraic techniques we obtain the following result.

Proposition 3.5.2 Let $0 < \alpha < \frac{1}{2}$ and $\delta = \pi_0^m - \pi_0^e$.

(1) If $\delta \leqslant 0$, then $\forall \alpha$, $\pi_\alpha^m - \pi_\alpha^e < 0$.
(2) If $\delta > 0$, then $\forall \alpha$, $s_\alpha^e - s_\alpha^m < 0$.

Proof: By definition and some algebraic manipulations we find that

$$\pi_\alpha^m - \pi_\alpha^e = (1 - 2\alpha)(\pi_0^m - \pi_0^e) - (1 - 2\alpha)2\alpha[(1 - \alpha)(\pi_0^m - \tfrac{1}{2}) + p_1 p_2 p_3 - (1 - p_1)(1 - p_2)(1 - p_3)]$$

and

$$s_\alpha^e - s_\alpha^m = \pi_\alpha^m - \pi_\alpha^e - \delta$$
$$= (-2\alpha)(\pi_0^m - \pi_0^e) - (1 - 2\alpha)2\alpha \, [(1 - \alpha)(\pi_0^m - \tfrac{1}{2}) + p_1 p_2 p_3 - (1 - p_1)(1 - p_2)(1 - p_3)]$$

The proposition follows directly from the above equalities.

Proposition 3.5.2 implies that the superiority of the expert rule for $\alpha = 0$ is invariant to decisional sabotage. That is, $\pi_0^e > \pi_0^m$ implies $\pi_\alpha^e > \pi_\alpha^m$ for any α. Note that a similar conclusion did not hold true under the total loss of skills model of the previous section. The second part of the proposition establishes that the expert rule is always less sensitive to decisional sabotage relative to the simple majority rule provided $\pi_0^m > \pi_0^e$. Note that α is assumed to be less than $\frac{1}{2}$. Without this assumption the comparison between e and m is meaningless since if $\alpha \geqslant \frac{1}{2}$, then both π_α^e and π_α^m are smaller than $\frac{1}{2}$.

Decisional sabotage: Case 2

Suppose that a single saboteur only operates within our three-member group. Each individual is likely to be that saboteur with probability α. As in the previous case the saboteur's probability of choosing correctly is $(1 - p_i)$. Under these circumstances and assuming equally skilled individuals the following result holds.

Proposition 3.5.3 Let $p_1 = p_2 = p_3 = p$. Then $\forall \alpha, 0 < \alpha < \frac{1}{2}$, $\pi_\alpha^m > \pi_\alpha^e$ and $d(\pi_\alpha^m - \pi_\alpha^e)/d\alpha > 0$.

Proof: By definition

$$\pi_\alpha^m = (1 - \alpha)[p^3 + 3p^2(1 - p)] + \alpha[p^2(1 - p) + p^3 + 2p(1 - p)^2]$$
$$= \alpha[4p^3 - 6p^2 + 2p] + 3p^2 - 2p^3$$

$$\pi_\alpha^e = p - \alpha(2p - 1)$$

$$\pi_\alpha^m - \pi_\alpha^e = \alpha[4p^3 - 6p^2 + 4p - 1] + 3p^2 - 2p^3 - p$$

$$\frac{d(\pi_\alpha^m - \pi_\alpha^e)}{d\alpha} = 4p^3 - 6p^2 + 4p - 1 > 0$$

$$\pi_0^m - \pi_0^e = \delta$$
$$= 3p^2 - 2p^3 - p$$
$$= p(2p - 1)(1 - p) > 0$$

From Proposition 3.5.3 we can conclude that the relative sensitivity of the expert rule $s_\alpha^e - s_\alpha^m$ increases with α so that the superiority of majority rule over the expert rule remains unchallenged for every α.

Complete information regarding individual skills is certainly a strong assumption, as we shall see in the medical application of Section 10.2. The next proposition assumes an extreme case of potential variability of skills where no information is available regarding the individual eventual decisional skills. Whereas the analysis based on our previous partial information assumptions does not lead to simple clear-cut general resolution of either the optimality or the sensitivity issues, here the optimality issue is unequivocably resolved. Simple majority rule is always preferable to the expert rule provided that the latter is considered as equivalent to an even-chance lottery on actual decisional skills.

Proposition 3.5.4[5] $\pi^m > \bar{p}$

Proof: $\pi(m, \frac{1}{2}, p_2, p_3) = \frac{1}{2}[p_2 + p_3] < \pi(m, p_1, p_2, p_3) = \pi^m$

$\pi(m, p_1, \frac{1}{2}, p_3) = \frac{1}{2}[p_1 + p_3] < \pi(m, p_1, p_2, p_3) = \pi^m$

$\pi(m, p_1, p_2, \frac{1}{2}) = \frac{1}{2}[p_1 + p_2] < \pi(m, p_1, p_2, p_3) = \pi^m$

(see Table 3.1 column (4)). Hence the simple average of the left-hand side terms is also smaller than π^m, that is

$$\frac{\frac{1}{2}[p_2 + p_3] + \frac{1}{2}[p_1 + p_3] + \frac{1}{2}[p_1 + p_2])}{3} = \frac{p_1 + p_2 + p_3}{3}$$

$$= \bar{p} < \pi^m$$

CHAPTER 4

Asymmetric alternatives

4.1   Introduction

The symmetry assumption comprises two components. First, non-biasedness in favor or against any alternative in the sense that both alternatives are a priori equally probable of being correct. Second, symmetry with respect to the pay-offs associated with the two alternatives while proving the outcomes to be either correct or incorrect. Interpreting alternative a as the acceptance of a certain proposal and alternative b as the rejection of that proposal, these components of symmetry imply that the probability as well as the costs of type 1 and type 2 errors are both identical. The two components of the symmetry assumption are quite restrictive. The second symmetry component is very likely violated when one of the alternatives is reversible and the other is not (for example when a criminal jury has to choose between conviction which implies death penalty and acquittal which implies no punishment). Such symmetry is also especially implausible in situations where the two alternatives are respectively interpreted as action and inaction or marginal and drastic courses of action. Unbiasedness in the sense of the first component of the symmetry definition is also not a plausible assumption. Usually there exists an a priori bias in favor of one of the alternatives (typically the status quo), and it is traditionally justified on the basis of the belief that existing policies reflect successful past efforts to choose the socially correct alternatives. If alternative a is a rejection of some proposal deviating from the status quo, and alternative b is the adoption of that proposal, then the designer of the optimal decision-making system, as well as all members of N, might share a unanimous belief that alternative a is correct in some probability α that is larger than $\frac{1}{2}$.

In this chapter the symmetry assumption is relaxed; in Section 4.2 the a priori bias α in favor of one alternative, say alternative a, is explicitly introduced into the basic model. The second component of the symmetry assumption is also relaxed. That is, we no longer assume that the net pay-off associated with a correct choice is independent of whether alternative a or alternative b is the correct choice. Theorem 4.2.1 identifies the optimal DDR in the more general setup while taking into account the prior probability α and the pay-offs associated with the alternatives under the two possible states of world. This rule is, in fact, a weighted qualified majority rule. A special class of weighted qualified majority rules is the well-known class of qualified majority rules. Hence the generalization of the basic model in this chapter suggests a possible formal justification of qualified majority rules as being optimal decision processes. Section 4.3 then focuses on qualified majority rules and analyzes the interrelationships among the factors which determine the particular optimal qualified majority rule in the special case where only the second component of the symmetry assumption is retained. These factors are the size of the decision-making body, the skills of the decision makers and the a priori bias in favor of alternative a.

4.2   The extended model

Consider our group of individuals $N = \{1, \ldots, n\}$ facing the two alternatives a and b. As before, a decision profile $x = (x_1, \ldots, x_n)$ is the actual representation of the group members' views. Under the uncertain dichotomous choice model two states of the world are possible: either alternative a or b is the correct choice. Correctness is defined here in the following manner: suppose that the benefit associated with the selection of alternative a in state of nature a is given by $B(1:1)$. The benefit associated with the selection of alternative a in state of nature b is given by $B(1:-1)$. Similarly, we have the two remaining benefits $B(-1:1)$ and $B(-1:1)$. Given state of nature a, alternative a is referred to as correct if $B(1:1) > B(-1:1)$. Given state of nature b, alternative b is the correct choice if $B(-1:-1) > B(1:-1)$. The members of N are interested in expected utility maximization. Their common utility is given in our specific context by the pay-off matrix

$$B = \begin{bmatrix} B(1:1) & B(-1:1) \\ B(1:-1) & B(-1:-1) \end{bmatrix}$$

Suppose that α and $(1 - \alpha)$, $0 \leqslant \alpha \leqslant 1$, are the a priori probabilities for the occurrence of state of nature a and state of nature b respectively, that is, α and $(1 - \alpha)$ are the priors that a and b are the correct alternatives. In such a situation we can interpret the prior as an additional voter, an $n + 1$ individual, who always supports alternative a. If alternative a is the status quo and $\alpha > \frac{1}{2}$, then voter $n + 1$ can be considered as a 'petrified' or 'phantom' voter representing the wisdom of past generations, i.e. the bias in favor of the status quo.

The decisional skill of an individual i is parameterized by the probability that he chooses correctly given that either alternative a or alternative b is the correct choice. These probabilities are denoted respectively by $p_i(1) = \text{Pr}(1:1)$ and $p_i(-1) = \text{Pr}(-1:-1)$. We now make the following three assumptions with respect to these probabilities:

For any consultant i, $\text{Pr}(-1:1) = 1 - p_i(1)$ and $\text{Pr}(1:-1) = 1 - p_i(-1)$. This assumption rules out the possibility of various courses of action such as individual i abstaining. An individual satisfying this assumption is decisively supporting either of the available alternatives and is therefore called decisive.

The second assumption requires that for any individual i, $p_i(1) = p_i(-1) = p_i$. That is, individual decisional skills are independent of the particular state of nature and, hence, can be represented by the single parameter p_i. Finally, individual decisional skills, the values of p_i, are assumed to be statistically independent.

The final selection of one of the available alternatives is made by means of a decisive decision rule. As in the basic model, we still ignore differences among decision rules that are based on the possibly different costs associated with the operation of the rules. We assume that such costs are identically equal to zero.

Our group is assumed to select a decisive decision rule that maximizes expected benefit. In order to formally define the objective function, we need to present the conditional probabilities for making a correct choice. For that purpose, let us partition the set of all possible decision profiles Ω into $X(1,f)$ and $X(-1,f)$ where $X(1,f) = \{x \in \Omega: f(x) = 1\}$ and $X(-1,f) = \{x \in \Omega: f(x) = -1\}$. For a given rule f, the group chooses correctly provided that a or b is the correct alternative with probability $\pi(f:1)$ or $\pi(f:-1)$ where $\pi(f:1) = \text{Pr}\{x \in X(1,f): 1\}$ and $\pi(f:-1) = \text{Pr}\{x \in X(-1,f): -1\}$. Since f is a decisive decision rule

$$\text{Pr}\{x \in X(-1, f):1\} = 1 - \pi(f:1)$$

and

$$\text{Pr}\{x \in X(1, f): -1\} = 1 - \pi(f:-1)$$

The general problem on which we focus is the maximization of expected benefit E over the set F of all decisive decision rules. Specifically, given the decision profile x, the prior α, the pay-off matrix B and decisional skills $(p_1, \ldots, p_n)$

$$(4.2.1) \quad \max_{f \in F} E(f; x, p_1, \ldots, p_n, \alpha, B)$$

Here

$$\begin{aligned}
E &= B(1:1)\pi(f:1)\alpha + B(-1:1)[1 - \pi(f:1)]\alpha \\
&\quad + B(-1:1)\pi(f:-1)(1 - \alpha) + B(1:-1)[1 - \pi(f:-1)](1 - \alpha) \\
&= B(1)\pi(f:1)\alpha + B(-1)\pi(f:-1)(1 - \alpha) \\
&\quad + [B(-1:1)\alpha + B(1:-1)(1 - \alpha)]
\end{aligned}$$

where $B(1) = B(1:1) - B(-1:1)$ is the alternative benefit, or the net benefit, associated with a correct choice, given that alternative a is correct. Similarly, $B(-1) = B(-1:1) - B(1:1)$. Denoting by $\hat{f}$ a solution to problem (4.2.1), we can now state the more general result.

Theorem 4.2.1

$$\hat{f} = \text{sign}\left(\sum_{i=1}^{n} \beta_i x_i + \gamma + \delta \right)$$

where

$$\beta_i = \ln \frac{p_i}{1 - p_i}$$

$$\gamma = \ln \frac{\alpha}{1 - \alpha}$$

and

$$\delta = \ln \frac{B(1)}{B(-1)}$$

Proof: For any decision profile x in Ω define a partition of the group members $1, 2, \ldots, n$ into $A(x)$ and $B(x)$ such that $i \in A(x)$ if $x_i = 1$ and $i \in B(x)$ if $x_i = -1$. Denote by $g(x:1)$ and $g(x:-1)$ the conditional probabilities to obtain x given that alternative a or b is the correct choice. That is

$$g(x:1) = \prod_{i \in A(x)} p_i \prod_{i \in B(x)} (1 - p_i)$$

and

$$g(x:-1) = \prod_{i \in B(x)} p_i \prod_{i \in A(x)} (1 - p_i)$$

For a given decision rule f

$$\pi(f:1) = \sum_{x \in X(1,f)} g(x:1)$$

and

$$\pi(f:-1) = \sum_{x \in X(-1,f)} g(x:-1)$$

By the definition of E, a sufficient condition for the optimality of the decision rule $\hat{f}$ is that

$$X(1, \hat{f}) = \{x : x \in \Omega \text{ and } B(1)g(x:1)\alpha > B(-1)g(x:-1)(1 - \alpha)\}$$

or equivalently

$$X(1,\hat{f}) = \left\{ x : x \in \Omega \text{ and } \frac{B(1)\alpha}{B(-1)(1-\alpha)} \prod_{i \in A(x)} p_i \prod_{i \in B(x)} (1-p_i) \right.$$

$$\left. > \prod_{i \in B(x)} p_i \prod_{i \in A(x)} (1-p_i) \right\}$$

$$= \left\{ x : x \in \Omega \text{ and } \frac{B(1)\alpha}{B(-1)(1-\alpha)} \prod_{i \in A(x)} \frac{p_i}{(1-p_i)} > \prod_{i \in B(x)} \frac{p_i}{(1-p_i)} \right\}$$

$$= \left\{ x : x \in \Omega \text{ and } \sum_{i \in A(x)} \beta_i + \gamma + \delta > \sum_{i \in B(x)} \beta_i \right\}$$

$$= \left\{ x : x \in \Omega \text{ and } \sum_{i} \beta_i x_i + \gamma + \delta > 0 \right\}$$

$$X(-1,\hat{f}) = \Omega - X(1,\hat{f}) = \left\{ x : x \in \Omega \text{ and } \sum_{i} \beta_i x_i + \gamma + \delta < 0 \right\}$$

So that

$$\hat{f} = \text{sign}\left(\sum_{i} \beta_i x_i + \gamma + \delta \right)$$

The optimal decision rule turns out to be a weighted qualified majority rule. The optimal experts' weights are proportional to the log odds of their decisional competences, the values of β_i. The particular qualified majority required depends on the log odds of the prior γ and on the log ratio between the net benefits under the two possible states of the world δ. A DDR f is called a weighted qualified majority rule f_q, if

$$f_q(x) = \begin{cases} -1 & -\left(\sum_{i=1}^{n} \beta_i x_i \right) \Big/ \left(\sum_{i=1}^{n} \beta_i \right) \geq q \\ \\ 1 & \text{otherwise} \end{cases}$$

That is, alternative b is chosen ($f_q(x) = -1$) if the normalized weighted advantage of b over a

$$-\left(\sum_{i=1}^{n} \beta_i x_i \right) \Big/ \sum_{i=1}^{n} \beta_i$$

exceeds the quota q. Theorem 4.2.1 directly implies that the optimal rule is a weighted qualified majority rule. Specifically:

Corollary 4.2.1 (1) The optimal rule $\hat{f}(p)$ is a weighted qualified majority rule, $f_{\hat{q}}$, with

$$\hat{q} = (\gamma + \delta) \Big/ \sum_{i=1}^{n} \beta_i \quad \text{where} \quad \beta_i = \ln\frac{p_i}{(1 - p_i)},$$

$$\gamma = \ln\frac{\alpha}{(1 - \alpha)} \quad \text{and} \quad \delta = \ln\frac{B(1)}{B(-1)}$$

Proof:

$$\hat{f}(p) = \text{sign}\left(\sum_{i=1}^{n} \beta_i x_i + \gamma + \delta \right)$$

That is, for a given profile x

$$\hat{f}(x) = \begin{cases} -1 & \sum_{i=1}^{n} \beta_i x_i + \gamma + \delta < 0 \\ 1 & \sum_{i=1}^{n} \beta_i x_i + \gamma + \delta > 0 \end{cases}$$

or

$$\hat{f}(x) = \begin{cases} -1 & \sum_{i=1}^{n} \beta_i x_i < -(\gamma + \delta) \\ 1 & \sum_{i=1}^{n} \beta_i x_i > -(\gamma + \delta) \end{cases}$$

or

$$\hat{f}(x) = \begin{cases} -1 & -\Sigma\beta_i x_i / \Sigma\beta_i > (\gamma + \delta)/\Sigma\beta_i = \hat{q} \\ 1 & \text{otherwise} \end{cases}$$

The optimal rule $f_{\hat{q}}$ is not a degenerate qualified majority rule only if

$$\beta' < \gamma + \delta < \sum_{i=1}^{n} \beta_i \quad \text{where} \quad \beta' = \min_i \beta_i$$

If

$$\gamma + \delta > \sum_{i=1}^{n} \beta_i$$

then $\hat{q} > 1$ and $f_{\hat{q}}(x) = 1$ for any decision profile x. That is, the status quo (alternative a) is always selected. If $\gamma + \delta < \beta'$, then

$$\hat{q} \sum_{i=1}^{n} \beta_i < \beta'$$

and

$$\text{sign}\left(\sum_{i=1}^{n} \beta_i x_i + \gamma + \delta \right) = \text{sign}\left(\sum_{i=1}^{n} \beta_i x_i + \hat{q} \sum_{i=1}^{n} \beta_i \right) = \text{sign}\left(\sum_{i=1}^{n} \beta_i x_i \right).$$

That is, the optimal rule is a weighted majority rule as in Theorem 2.3.1. Note that $\gamma + \delta = 0$ when $\alpha B(1) = (1 - \alpha)B(-1)$ and, in particular, when $\alpha = \frac{1}{2}$ and $B(1) = B(-1)$. Clearly, in such a case $\hat{f} = \text{sign}(\sum_{i=1}^{n} \beta_i x_i)$. Under this latter case the two types of asymmetry are balanced and the resulting optimal decision rule is a weighted majority rule.

An interesting special case of Corollary 4.2.1 (1) is obtained when voters are equally skilled, i.e. $p_i = p$ for every i in N. Assigning the same p to all decision makers can be justified by the inability to take into account special information regarding the different persons at the stage when the decision system is designed (for instance, at the constitutional stage). In this special case the optimal DDR is a standard qualified majority rule.

A DDR f is called a qualified majority rule f_r if

$$f_r(x) = \begin{cases} -1 & \left(-\sum_{i=1}^{n} x_i\right)\Big/n \geqslant r \\ 1 & \text{otherwise} \end{cases}$$

Let $N(a)$ and $N(b)$ denote the number of decision makers voting for alternative a and alternative b respectively $(N(a) + N(b) = n)$. Under a qualified majority rule alternative b is chosen if the average advantage of b over a

$$\frac{N(b) - N(a)}{n} = \frac{-\sum_{i=1}^{n} x_i}{n}$$

exceeds the quota r. By Corollary 4.2.1 (1), for individuals with equal decisional skills, the optimal rule is a qualified majority rule f_r with a quota that is equal to the ratio between $(\gamma + \delta)$ and $n\beta$, i.e.

$$\hat{r} = \frac{(\gamma + \delta)}{n\beta} \quad \text{where} \quad \gamma = \ln\frac{\alpha}{(1 - \alpha)}, \quad \delta = \ln\frac{B(1)}{B(-1)} \quad \text{and} \quad \beta = \ln\frac{p}{(1 - p)}$$

An alternative and more common definition of qualified majority rules is the following one.

A DDR f is called a qualified majority rule f_k if

$$f_k(x) = \begin{cases} -1 & N(b) \geqslant kn \\ 1 & \text{otherwise} \end{cases}$$

That is, alternative b is selected when the number of decision makers voting for b is larger than kn, $\frac{1}{2} \leqslant k \leqslant 1$.

A qualified majority rule retains a formal equality of authority among the decision makers, but it requires the assent of more than a simple majority for the imposition of new policies. Thus, such a rule gives, in fact, special authority to individuals who happen to support alternative a, the status quo.

Alternatively, the rule gives an advantage to the status quo and in this sense it is a conservative rule, which protects minority judgements. For example, a two-thirds qualified majority rule allows a minority of just over one-third to frustrate the judgements of a majority of just under two-thirds, provided that the minority members are nay-sayers voting for a, the majority are yea-sayers voting for b. The following corollary identifies the optimal qualified majority rule using the alternative definition f_k.

Corollary 4.2.1 (2) The optimal rule $\hat{f}(p)$ for equally skilled individuals is a qualified majority rule $f_{\hat{k}}$, where

$$\hat{k} = \tfrac{1}{2}\left[1 + \frac{\gamma + \delta}{\beta n}\right] = \tfrac{1}{2}[1 + \hat{r}]$$

Proof: Let $\beta_0 = \gamma + \delta$. Note that

$$2\beta[n\hat{k} - N(b)] = 2n\beta\left[\frac{1}{2}\left(1 + \frac{\beta_0}{\beta n}\right) - \frac{N(b)}{n}\right]$$

$$= \beta\left[n - 2N(b) + \frac{\beta_0}{\beta}\right]$$

$$= \beta\left[N(a) - N(b) + \frac{\beta_0}{\beta}\right]$$

$$= \beta[N(a) - N(b)] + \beta_0$$

Hence

$$2[n\hat{k} - N(b)] = N(a) - N(b) + \frac{\beta_0}{\beta}$$

Clearly

$$n\hat{k} - N(b) \leqslant 0 \leftrightarrow N(b) \geqslant \hat{k}n$$

$$\leftrightarrow N(a) - N(b) + \frac{\beta_0}{\beta} \leqslant 0$$

$$\leftrightarrow N(b) - N(a) \leqslant \frac{\beta_0}{\beta}$$

$$\leftrightarrow -\left(\sum_{i=1}^{n} x_i\right)\bigg/ n \leqslant \frac{\beta_0}{n\beta}$$

To sum up

$$N(b) \geqslant \hat{k}n \leftrightarrow -\left(\sum_{i=1}^{n} x_i\right)\bigg/ n \geqslant \frac{\beta_0}{n\beta} = \frac{\gamma + \delta}{n\beta} = \hat{r}$$

and so

$$f_{\hat{k}} = f_{\hat{r}}$$

Qualified majority rules have enjoyed a special place in the ideological tradition of contemporary liberal democracy. Although a simple majority is the rule most often used, qualified majority rules are also common. For example, an amendment to the Constitution of the United States requires ratification by three-fourths of the State legislatures before it becomes law, assuming that the amendment has passed each house of Congress by a two-thirds vote. In France, a three-fifths majority of the 'Congress of Parliament' (a joint session of the Senate and National Assembly) is required to modify the Constitution. In Israel, certain sections of the Basic Law may be amended or modified only by a special majority of two-thirds. Within certain committees of the Israeli Parliament (the Knesset), a four-fifths majority is necessary to approve the policies of certain government agencies.

While a sizable technical literature has grown up in economics and political science analyzing the merits of a simple majority rule (see, for instance, Buchanan and Tullock (1962), Fishburn (1973), Rae (1969), Schofield (1972), Sen (1970), Straffin (1977)), no similar effort has been made concerning the investigation of qualified majority rules (see, however, Buchanan and Tullock (1962), in particular, Ch. 15, and Rae (1969), in particular, Section III). Corollary 4.2.1 (2) partly corrects this imbalance. It provides a possible formal justification of qualified majority rules claiming that whenever voters are equally skilled such rules are optimal. The special majority needed is given by

$$\frac{1}{2}\left[1 + \frac{\gamma + \delta}{n\beta}\right]$$

The following implications are directly obtained from Corollary 4.2.1 (2). First for sufficiently qualified decision makers, or for a sufficiently large decision-making body, or for a sufficiently small bias, the optimal decision rule is the simple majority rule, i.e. $\hat{k} = \frac{1}{2}$. Second, if $\beta_0 = \gamma + \delta > n\beta$, then the optimal decision rule selects alternative a, the status quo, under any voting profile x, i.e. $\hat{k} > 1$. Note that in such a case

$$\ln\frac{\alpha}{1 - \alpha} + \ln\frac{B(1)}{B(-1)} > n \ln\frac{p}{1 - p}$$

i.e. the total net weight assigned to the status quo is larger than the sum of weights assigned to the decision makers. Therefore, an optimal qualified majority rule is non-degenerate ($\hat{k} \leqslant 1$) if either p or n are large enough. For instance, if p tends to $\frac{1}{2}$, and therefore β tends to zero, and $\alpha > \frac{1}{2}$, $B(1) > B(-1)$, then the degenerate rule ($\hat{k} > 1$) is obtained for any finite n. Finally, Theorem

4.2.1 provides direct insight into the issue of democracy versus rule by the select few. For instance, in an analogous manner to the three corollaries of Theorem 2.3.1, Theorem 4.2.1 can be used to find under what circumstances the collective decision should be made by a subgroup of N, and, in particular, by the most skillful individual, and under what circumstances the simple majority rule is the optimal procedure.

4.3   The optimality of qualified majority rules: skills, size and bias

The optimal qualified majority rule for equally skilled individuals depends on four variables: first, the size of the decision-making body; second, the skills of the decision makers; third, the a priori bias in favor of the status quo; fourth, the ratio between the net benefits $B(1)$ and $B(-1)$. If $B(1) = B(-1)$, then

$$\hat{f} = \text{sign}\left(\sum_{i=1}^{n} b_i x_i + \gamma \right)$$

In this partially symmetric case the fourth variable can be ignored as

$$\ln \frac{B(1)}{B(-1)} = \delta = 0$$

We conclude this chapter by focusing on the relationships among the three variables α, p and n in determining the optimal qualified majority rule $f_{\hat{k}}$, assuming that $\delta = 0$. Table 4.1, which is based on the qualified majority rule theorem, shows the optimal special majorities corresponding to various combinations of α and p for six typical group sizes, $n = 5, 9, 12, 21, 120$ and 435. For example, in a committee of five members with $p = 0.70$ and $\alpha = 0.70$, the optimal qualified majority rule is the three-fifths rule; that is, alternative b is chosen if at least three individuals vote for it ($\hat{k} = 0.60$).

Note that n is an integer but nk is not necessarily so. For any real number r denote by **r** the smallest integer that is larger or equal to r. By the definition of qualified majority rules, two such rules f_k and $f_{k'}$ are identical ($f_k(x) = f_{k'}(x)$ for every decision profile x) whenever **nk** is equal to **nk'**. For example, if $n = 5$ the minimal number of supporters required to select alternative b (and consisting of a majority) can be three, four or five. In turn, if k and k' satisfy **nk** = **nk'**, such that this common integer can be equal to three, four or five, then $f_k = f_{k'}$. Alternatively, if both k and k' satisfy $0.40 < k, k' \leqslant 0.60$, or $0.60 < k, k' \leqslant 0.80$, or $0.80 < k, k' \leqslant 1$, then f_k and $f_{k'}$ are identical qualified majority rules. In the matrices corresponding to $n = 5$, 9 and 12, identical qualified majority rules belong to the same region, where distinct regions are bordered by the dotted lines. For instance, in a committee of five decision makers, if $\alpha = 0.85$ and $p = 0.70$, then the seven-tenths majority rule is optimal ($\hat{k} = 0.70$). Indeed, this rule is optimal for any p satisfying $0.65 < p < 0.80$ as in all of these cases $n\hat{k} = 3$.

In a twelve-person criminal trial jury, the requirement of unanimity for conviction is optimal, provided that the members are moderately skilled and there is a very high prior in favor of acquittal (for example, suppose $\alpha = 0.90$ and $p = 0.55$ or $\alpha = 0.99$ and $p = 0.60$). In general, the jury rule emerges as the optimal rule if

$$\tfrac{11}{12} \leqslant \hat{k} \leqslant \tfrac{12}{12}$$

By Corollary 4.2.1 (2), the jury rule is optimal whenever

$$\frac{11}{12} \leqslant \frac{1}{2}\left[1 + \frac{\ln(\alpha/1 - \alpha)}{12\ln(p/1 - p)} \right] \leqslant \frac{12}{12}$$

or

$$\frac{5}{12} \leqslant \frac{\ln(\alpha/1 - \alpha)}{24\ln(p/1 - p)} \leqslant \frac{6}{12}$$

or

$$10 \leqslant \frac{\ln(\alpha/1 - \alpha)}{\ln(p/1 - p)} \leqslant 12$$

Obviously, the assumption of independence among individual decisions has its immediate drawbacks in this particular context.

In the United States House of Representatives ($n = 435$), or in the Israeli Knesset ($n = 120$), n is sufficiently large to ensure the optimality of simple majority rule (see Table 4.1 where all values of $\hat{k}$ corresponding to $n = 435$ or $n = 120$ and any combination of α and p are equal either to 0.50 or 0.51). Put differently, the qualified majority rule theorem implies that the common special majority rules, such as the two-thirds or three-fifths rules, are bad choices for such large decision-making bodies. Again, in this context, independence among individual voters is an unreasonable assumption. However, it is more reasonable to assume independence among voters of different political factions even if votes are dependent within each faction. Under this alternative assumption the desirability of certain special majority rules can be restored because the number of decision makers is actually reduced from n to the number of factions in the decision-making body. Finally, observe that $\hat{k} = \tfrac{1}{2}$ if $p > \alpha$; that is, $\hat{k} = \tfrac{1}{2}$ for all entries above the diagonal, and, in addition, as n increases, the appeal of the simple majority rule also increases.

The substitutability among skill p, bias α and size n in generating a particular optimal qualified majority rule, given that $B(1) = B(-1)$, can be directly obtained from Corollary 4.2.1 (2). The trade-off between skill p and a

Table 4.1. The optimal special majority (k̂) as a function of number of decision makers (n) skills (p) and a priori bias (α).

$n = 5$

α \ p	0.55	0.60	0.65	0.70	0.75	0.80	0.85	0.90	0.95	0.99
0.55	0.60	0.55	0.53	0.52	0.52	0.51	0.51	0.51	0.51	0.50
0.60	0.70	0.60	0.57	0.55	0.54	0.53	0.52	0.52	0.51	0.51
0.65	0.81	0.65	0.60	0.57	0.56	0.54	0.54	0.53	0.52	0.51
0.70	0.92	0.71	0.64	0.60	0.58	0.56	0.55	0.54	0.53	0.52
0.75	1.05	0.77	0.68	0.63	0.60	0.58	0.56	0.55	0.54	0.52
0.80	1.19	0.84	0.72	0.65	0.63	0.60	0.58	0.56	0.55	0.53
0.85	1.36	0.93	0.78	0.70	0.66	0.63	0.60	0.58	0.56	0.54
0.90	1.59	1.04	0.85	0.76	0.70	0.66	0.63	0.60	0.57	0.55
0.95	1.97	1.23	0.98	0.85	0.77	0.71	0.67	0.63	0.60	0.56
0.99	2.79	1.63	1.24	1.04	0.92	0.83	0.76	0.71	0.66	0.60

$n = 9$

α \ p	0.55	0.60	0.65	0.70	0.75	0.80	0.85	0.90	0.95	0.99
0.55	0.56	0.53	0.52	0.51	0.51	0.51	0.51	0.51	0.50	0.50
0.60	0.61	0.56	0.54	0.53	0.52	0.52	0.51	0.51	0.51	0.50
0.65	0.67	0.58	0.56	0.54	0.53	0.52	0.52	0.52	0.51	0.51
0.70	0.73	0.62	0.58	0.56	0.54	0.53	0.53	0.52	0.52	0.51
0.75	0.80	0.65	0.60	0.57	0.56	0.54	0.54	0.53	0.52	0.51
0.80	0.88	0.69	0.62	0.59	0.56	0.54	0.54	0.53	0.52	0.52
0.85	0.98	0.74	0.66	0.61	0.59	0.56	0.56	0.54	0.53	0.52
0.90	1.11	0.80	0.70	0.64	0.61	0.59	0.57	0.56	0.54	0.53
0.95	1.32	0.90	0.76	0.69	0.65	0.62	0.59	0.57	0.56	0.56
0.99	1.77	1.13	0.91	0.80	0.73	0.68	0.65	0.62	0.59	0.56

$n = 12$

α \ p	0.55	0.60	0.65	0.70	0.75	0.80	0.85	0.90	0.95	0.99
0.55	0.54	0.52	0.51	0.51	0.51	0.50	0.50	0.50	0.50	0.50
0.60	0.58	0.54	0.53	0.52	0.52	0.51	0.51	0.51	0.51	0.50
0.65	0.63	0.56	0.54	0.53	0.52	0.51	0.51	0.51	0.51	0.51
0.70	0.68	0.59	0.56	0.54	0.53	0.52	0.52	0.52	0.51	0.51
0.75	0.73	0.61	0.57	0.55	0.53	0.53	0.52	0.52	0.52	0.51
0.80	0.79	0.64	0.59	0.57	0.54	0.53	0.53	0.53	0.52	0.51
0.85	0.86	0.68	0.62	0.59	0.57	0.55	0.54	0.53	0.52	0.52
0.90	0.96	0.73	0.65	0.61	0.58	0.57	0.55	0.54	0.53	0.52
0.95	1.11	0.80	0.70	0.64	0.61	0.59	0.57	0.56	0.54	0.53
0.99	1.45	0.97	0.81	0.73	0.67	0.64	0.61	0.59	0.57	0.54

$n = 21$

α \ p	0.55	0.60	0.65	0.70	0.75	0.80	0.85	0.90	0.95	0.99
0.55	0.52	0.51	0.51	0.51	0.50	0.50	0.50	0.50	0.50	0.50
0.60	0.55	0.52	0.52	0.51	0.51	0.51	0.51	0.50	0.50	0.50
0.65	0.57	0.54	0.52	0.52	0.51	0.51	0.51	0.51	0.51	0.50
0.70	0.60	0.55	0.53	0.52	0.52	0.51	0.51	0.51	0.51	0.50
0.75	0.63	0.56	0.54	0.53	0.52	0.52	0.52	0.51	0.51	0.51
0.80	0.66	0.58	0.55	0.54	0.53	0.52	0.52	0.52	0.51	0.51
0.85	0.71	0.60	0.57	0.55	0.54	0.53	0.52	0.52	0.51	0.51
0.90	0.76	0.63	0.58	0.56	0.55	0.54	0.53	0.52	0.52	0.51
0.95	0.85	0.67	0.61	0.58	0.56	0.55	0.54	0.53	0.52	0.52
0.99	1.05	0.77	0.68	0.63	0.60	0.58	0.56	0.55	0.54	0.52

$n = 120$

α \ p	0.55	0.60	0.65	0.70	0.75	0.80	0.85	0.90	0.95	0.99
0.55	0.50	0.50	0.50	0.50	0.50	0.50	0.50	0.50	0.50	0.50
0.60	0.51	0.50	0.50	0.50	0.50	0.50	0.50	0.50	0.50	0.50
0.65	0.51	0.51	0.50	0.50	0.50	0.50	0.50	0.50	0.50	0.50
0.70	0.52	0.51	0.51	0.50	0.50	0.50	0.50	0.50	0.50	0.50
0.75	0.52	0.51	0.51	0.51	0.50	0.50	0.50	0.50	0.50	0.50
0.80	0.53	0.51	0.51	0.51	0.51	0.50	0.50	0.50	0.50	0.50
0.85	0.54	0.52	0.51	0.51	0.51	0.51	0.50	0.50	0.50	0.50
0.90	0.55	0.52	0.51	0.51	0.51	0.51	0.51	0.50	0.50	0.50
0.95	0.56	0.53	0.52	0.51	0.51	0.51	0.51	0.51	0.50	0.50
0.99	0.60	0.55	0.53	0.52	0.52	0.51	0.51	0.51	0.51	0.50

$n = 435$

α \ p	0.55	0.60	0.65	0.70	0.75	0.80	0.85	0.90	0.95	0.99
0.55	0.50	0.50	0.50	0.50	0.50	0.50	0.50	0.50	0.50	0.50
0.60	0.50	0.50	0.50	0.50	0.50	0.50	0.50	0.50	0.50	0.50
0.65	0.50	0.50	0.50	0.50	0.50	0.50	0.50	0.50	0.50	0.50
0.70	0.50	0.50	0.50	0.50	0.50	0.50	0.50	0.50	0.50	0.50
0.75	0.51	0.50	0.50	0.50	0.50	0.50	0.50	0.50	0.50	0.50
0.80	0.51	0.50	0.50	0.50	0.50	0.50	0.50	0.50	0.50	0.50
0.85	0.51	0.50	0.50	0.50	0.50	0.50	0.50	0.50	0.50	0.50
0.90	0.51	0.51	0.50	0.50	0.50	0.50	0.50	0.50	0.50	0.50
0.95	0.52	0.51	0.51	0.51	0.50	0.50	0.50	0.50	0.50	0.50
0.99	0.53	0.51	0.51	0.51	0.50	0.50	0.50	0.50	0.50	0.50

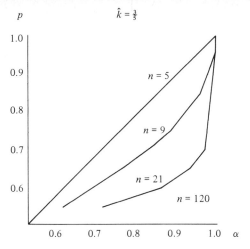

Figure 4.1. The optimality of three-fifths majority rule ($\hat{k} = \frac{3}{5}$) in *n*-members decision bodies ($n = 5, 9, 21, 120$) for various skills p and a priori α.

priori bias α in engendering a particular optimal special majority $\hat{k}$ for a given size of decision-making body n is explicitly given by

$$\alpha = \frac{p^m}{(1-p)^m + p^m}$$

such that

$$m = 2n(\hat{k} - \tfrac{1}{2})$$

Similarly, the trade-off between α and n for a particular $\hat{k}$ and p is given by

$$\alpha = \frac{\exp(ny)}{1 + \exp(ny)}$$

such that

$$y = 2\beta(\hat{k} - \tfrac{1}{2})$$

And, the trade-off between p and n for a particular $\hat{k}$ and α is given by

$$p = \frac{\exp(x/n)}{1 + \exp(x/n)}$$

such that

$$x = \frac{\gamma}{2(\hat{k} - \tfrac{1}{2})}$$

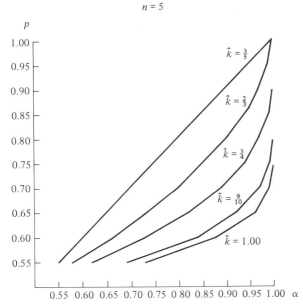

Figure 4.2. The optimality of special majority rules ($\hat{k} = \frac{3}{5}, \frac{2}{3}, \frac{3}{4}, \frac{9}{10}, 1$) in a five-member body for various skills p and bias α.

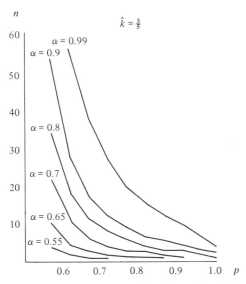

Figure 4.3. The optimality of special majority rule ($\hat{k} = \frac{3}{5}$) under fixed biases ($\alpha = 0.55, 0.65, 0.7, 0.8, 0.9, 0.99$) for various skills p and numbers of decision makers n.

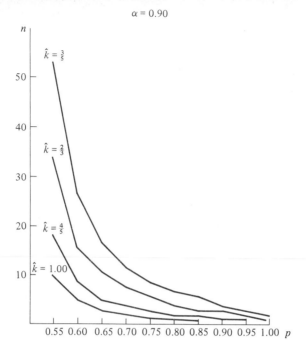

Figure 4.4. The optimality of qualified majority rules ($\hat{k} = \frac{3}{5}, \frac{2}{3}, \frac{4}{5}, 1$) for $\alpha = 0.9$ and various values of p and n.

Figures 4.1–4.4 present iso-optimal special majority curves. Figure 4.1 shows the trade-off between skill and bias for a three-fifths special majority rule under fixed sizes of decision-making bodies. Figure 4.2 shows the trade-off between skill and bias in a five-member body for six special majority rules. The curves in Figures 4.1 and 4.2 are positively sloped. That is, skill and bias are positively related along iso-optimal special majority curves. In Figure 4.1, under $\hat{k} = \frac{3}{5}$, as the size of the decision-making body is increased, the iso-optimal special majority curves shift in a south-easterly direction. For a sufficiently large n the curves disappear. That is, no combination of skill and bias justifies $\hat{k}$ as an optimal decision rule. For instance, if $n \geqslant 120$, a special majority larger than 0.6 never emerges as an optimum rule. With a given size of decision-making body, as k increases the iso-optimal special majority curves again shift in a south-east direction (see Figure 4.2, in which $n = 5$).

Figure 4.3 shows the trade-off between skill and the number of decision makers for the three-fifths common special majority rule under certain fixed a priori biases. Figure 4.4 shows the trade-off between skill and the number of decision makers for four qualified majority rules, assuming that $\alpha = 0.90$.

The curves in Figures 4.3 and 4.4 are negatively sloped. That is, skill and size are negatively related along iso-optimal special majority curves. In Figure 4.3, under $\hat{k} = 3/5$, as the a priori bias in favor of the status quo is decreased, the iso-optimal special majority curves shift in a south-westerly direction. Under a given bias, as $\hat{k}$ is increased, the iso-optimal special majority curves again shift in a south-westerly direction (see Figure 4.4, in which $\alpha = 0.9$).

Consider a particular decision-making body that uses a certain special rule k_0. Within our framework, this body is fully characterized by its size, skill and bias, that is, by the triple (n, p, α). Table 4.1, together with Figures 4.1–4.4, demonstrate precisely the circumstances under which this body selects a special majority rule that is too restrictive (k_0 is too large). In diagrammatic terms, such a selection occurs if the decision-making body is characterized by a point that lies above the k_0 iso-optimal curve. In general, the prospect of k_0 being too restrictive grows as the size of the decision-making body and the quality of the decision making increases, or as the bias in favor of the status quo decreases. For instance if $k_0 = \frac{3}{4}$, then for $n > 22$, even if $p \geqslant 0.6$ and $\alpha \leqslant 0.99$, k_0 is too restrictive. Or if $\alpha \leqslant 0.9$, $p > 0.65$ and $n > 17$, even a moderate special majority rule, for example the three-fourths majority rule, is too restrictive.

CHAPTER 5

Incomplete information on decisional skills

5.1   Introduction

Our study of optimal group judgemental processes in situations involving pairwise choice has so far assumed full information regarding the judgemental competences of the individual group members. (Recall that the decisional competences of members in N are measured by their probabilities of judging correctly, i.e. the values of p_i.) In particular, the identification of the optimal decision rule – the rule that maximizes the expected common utility of the decision makers – hinges upon the availability of information regarding the vector of skills $(p_1, \ldots, p_n)$. See, for example, Theorem 2.3.1 or Theorem 2.4.1.

The assumption of full information regarding decision makers' competences is very restricting as it is, of course, not always possible to determine or even estimate these competences. Some of the difficulties associated with competences estimation are discussed in Section 10.2. In other words, 'a serious drawback of the various versions of the uncertain dichotomous choice model is that they are predicated on probabilistic values that are probably not known' (Young, 1983). Although there are a few particular situations where decisional competence can be assessed (either directly on the basis of each individual's past decisional record as in the medical example discussed in Section 10.2 or indirectly by, for example, comparing each individual choice with those made by the group majority, see Grofman *et al.* (1983)), there seems to exist an urgent need to extend the basic uncertain dichotomous choice model by relaxing the full information assumption regarding the competences of the decision makers.

In the existing literature the only attempts to do this have been carried out either in the restricted context of Condorcet's Jury Theorem where the group decision rule is assumed to be simple majority rule, or in the context of comparing the performance of simple majority rule to that of the expert rule (dictatorship of the most competent decision maker). For a summary of these attempts, see Grofman *et al.* (1983). Although the study of simple majority rule and the expert rule is of considerable interest, neither of these two rules need be the optimal rule.[1] Quite surprisingly, the more general optimality issue has not been analyzed under any partial information assumption whatsoever. The analysis of the general optimality issue is the main purpose of this chapter.

In the following section we discuss two possible basic forms of incomplete information regarding decisional competences. In the first case some direct information regarding the vector of skills $(p_1, \ldots, p_n)$ is available, however, this information is incomplete. We illustrate how the optimal rule can still be identified in some of these instances. In the second and more interesting case no direct information on $(p_1, \ldots, p_n)$ is available, however, there exists some information regarding the distribution of decisional competences in the population from which the individual members of N were drawn. The remainder of this chapter offers partial and complete analysis of the general optimality issue employing alternative assumptions regarding the distribution of decisional skills and regarding the size of the decision-making body. A partial analysis enables the evaluation of some, though not all, of the relevant rules, and in particular, only one such rule. In any event the evaluated rules are compared to *all* of the relevant rules. A complete analysis means that all relevant rules are evaluated.

Employing the necessary and sufficient condition for the optimality of the expert rule (Corollary 2.3.1 (2)) we derive in Section 5.3 the probability that this rule is optimal given that the individual odds of deciding correctly are log-normally distributed. The same condition is then used to estimate the optimality likelihood of the expert rule given that individual decisional competences are uniformly distributed. A complete optimality analysis requires the derivation of optimality probabilities for all relevant decision rules. Such an analysis is not even attempted here because the identification of all such relevant rules is an extremely complex task when the group size is sufficiently large. In contrast, the expert rule is always a relevant rule and the condition for its optimality is valid for any group size. We are able, however, to illustrate the fuller optimality analysis for the special case of five-member groups that is thoroughly discussed in Section 2.5. Assuming a uniform distribution of individual competences we estimate, in Section 5.4, the optimality probabilities of the seven weighted majority rules that are relevant in this case. Section 5.5 concludes by establishing the total inferiority of the expert rule in three-member groups assuming, first, complete ignorance regarding individual competences and, second, that the expert rule is equivalent to an even-chance lottery on individual skills.

5.2   Partial information on decisional skills

Consider a group of n individuals whose decisional skills are unknown. Suppose that these individuals constitute a random sample from a given population of decision makers and let our indirect partial information on the individual competences take the form of a particular distribution function of the variable p_i. That is, an individual decisional skill is treated as a random variable and information is available regarding its probability distribution. The availability of such information on decisional skills makes possible an optimality analysis resulting in the identification of the rule that is most likely to yield the largest expected utility, or, under our assumptions, the largest probability that the group chooses the correct alternative.

Although the optimal rule in the above sense can be identified, it is usually impossible to implement the optimal group strategy in this partial information case because competences of the decision makers are unknown and, therefore, the ranking of the values of p_i is also unknown. Without this ranking, application of the optimality analysis is infeasible. For example, suppose that the expert rule is likely to be the best rule. Then, without being able to identify the most competent individual, we cannot take advantage of the optimality result, i.e. apply the expert rule. Note, however, that if simple majority rule is most likely to be optimal, then the optimal group strategy would be to select that rule, and the implementation of this strategy does not require any further information on skills, and in particular, information regarding the ranking of the values of p_i. Furthermore, it is usually possible to estimate the actual individual decisional skills. Such an estimation is a costly process and our analysis might be helpful in clarifying to what extent investment in such an estimation process is warranted. Finally, it should be noted that very often decision-making bodies rigidly adhere to the usage of particular decision rules. For example, in many countries corporate boards are legally enforced to utilize the simple majority rule. Under such sub-optimal circumstances the analysis may contribute to the improvement of group decision making. That is, if for some reason the group is committing itself, say at the constitutional stage, to the employment of one particular decision mechanism, then certainly our partial information analysis clarifies what is the desirable strategy for the group, i.e. the analysis identifies the rule most likely to be the optimal one.

In the following sections we present three examples that illustrate how optimality analysis can be carried out under alternative assumptions on the distribution of individual decisional skills. Before turning to these examples, let us briefly mention an alternative form of partial information that might enable identification of optimal rules.

Suppose that some direct information regarding the decisional competences of individual members in N is available, but that the information is incomplete. For example, suppose that it is only known that members of N are equally skilled. Then, by direct application of Corollary 2.3.1 (3), we can deduce that simple majority rule is optimal, even though the exact vector of skills is unknown. Or, consider a trivial situation in which a particular individual is known to be an expert whose competence p_1 is equal to 1. Further information on $p_2, \ldots, p_n$ is not required as the expert rule is, obviously, the optimal rule (see Corollary 2.3.1 (2)). More meaningful examples can be constructed. For instance, for certain decision-making bodies it is possible to identify the optimal rule given information on the interval $[p_1, p_n]$. We do not pursue further the discussion of this alternative sort of partial information as it is both more limited in scope and less interesting than the former type.

5.3   Expert optimality

Our analysis in this section focuses on the expert rule where group decision is left in the hands of the most qualified decision maker, for two reasons. First, the expert rule is the only weighted majority rule that belongs to the set of weighted majority rules for any size of N, and, in particular, regardless of whether n is odd or even. Hence, although the optimality analysis carried out below depends on the particular partial information assumption we choose to make, it does not depend in principle on the size of the group. Second, and more importantly, necessary and sufficient conditions for the optimality of any rule are currently available only for the expert rule. Specifically, by Corollary 2.3.1 (2), the expert rule emerges as the optimal rule for any n-member group if and only if there exists an individual j such that

$$\beta_j > \sum_{i \neq j} \beta_i \quad \text{where} \quad \beta_i = \ln \frac{p_i}{(1 - p_i)}$$

This condition can be used to evaluate the expert rule under the milder conditions whereby only partial information is available regarding the decisional competences of the group members. This we illustrate assuming two particular competence distributions and employing, respectively, two different methodological approaches. Specifically, we derive analytically the likelihood of the expert rule being the optimal one when the odds of an individual's choosing correctly are log-normally distributed. We then employ a standard Monte Carlo simulation technique to compute the likelihood of the expert rule being the optimal one assuming that skills (the values of p_i) are uniformly distributed on the interval $[0.5, 1]$.

5.3.1 *Expert optimality under the log-normal distribution of individual odds of choosing correctly*

Suppose that β_i is normally distributed with mean μ and variance σ^2. That is, $\beta_i \sim N(\mu, \sigma^2)$.[2] For a group of n members randomly assembled from this

Table 5.1 *Approximate probability for the optimality of the expert rule P_e when $\beta_i \sim N(\mu, \sigma^2)$.*

$n \backslash \mu/\sigma$	0.6	0.8	1	1.5	2	3	4
3	0.9999	0.9684	0.8430	0.5847	0.3843	0.1254	0.0312
4	0.9999	0.8476	0.6348	0.2672	0.0912	0.0052	
5	0.9999	0.7115	0.4505	0.1110	0.0185		
6	0.9810	0.5808	0.3096	0.0426	0.0036		
7	0.9044	0.4585	0.2058	0.0287			
8	0.8960	0.3568	0.1360	0.0064			
9	0.7272	0.2763	0.0081	0.0018			

population we wish to compute the probability that there exists an individual j such that $\beta_j > \sum_{i \neq j} \beta_i$.[3] Denoting the approximated probability by P_e we obtain that

$$P_e = n \Pr \left\{ \sum_{i=2}^{n} \beta_i - \beta_1 \leq 0 \right\}$$

Let

$$\gamma = \sum_{i=2}^{n} \beta_i - \beta_1$$

and so

$$P_e = n \Pr \{ \gamma \leq 0 \}$$

By assumption, $\gamma \sim N((n-2)\mu, n\sigma^2)$, and therefore

$$P_e = n \Pr \left\{ \frac{\gamma - (n-2)\mu}{\sqrt{n}\sigma} \leq -\frac{(n-2)\mu}{\sqrt{n}\sigma} \right\} = n\phi \left(-\frac{\mu(n-2)}{\sigma\sqrt{n}} \right)$$

where $\phi(z)$ is the standardized normal distribution function. Table 5.1 displays the values of P_e corresponding to some combinations of n and μ/σ. For sufficiently large groups and sufficiently large mean-standard deviation ratios of β_i, the expert rule is certainly not the optimal rule.

In comparing the expert rule to simple majority rule, assuming that the values of p_i are normally distributed, Grofman (1978) reports that for intermediate average competency levels only in relatively small groups is democracy preferred to rule by dictatorship of the most competent member. A similar conclusion cannot be confirmed here, where the expert rule is compared to all other alternative rules and not merely to simple majority rule and where β_i is assumed to be normal. In fact, even for three-member groups this conclusion is refuted in our case despite the fact that the expert rule and

Table 5.2 *Estimated likelihood for the optimality of the expert rule P_e when p_i is uniformly distributed on* $[0.5,1]$.

n	3	4	5	6	7	8	9
P_e	0.673	0.385	0.201	0.101	0.053	0.027	0.007

simple majority rule are the only two relevant weighted majority rules when $n = 3$.

5.3.2 *Expert optimality under uniform distribution of competences*

Suppose that p_i is uniformly distributed between 0.5 and 1. Employing the necessary and sufficient condition for the optimality of the expert rule and a standard Monte Carlo routine, we have generated 1000 populations of size n with skills drawn from the above uniform distribution and determined for each population whether the condition

$$\beta_j \geqslant \sum_{i \neq j} \beta_i$$

is satisfied for some j. Our findings are shown in Table 5.2 where the estimated likelihood for the optimality of the expert rule P_e is computed for n-member groups, $3 \leqslant n \leqslant 9$. In a three-member group the expert rule is more likely to be the optimal rule than simple majority rule, which is the only alternative relevant weighted majority rule. That is, for $n = 3$ the best individual performance within the group is usually superior to the group's performance. In order to resolve the same issue (comparing the expert rule to the group's performance) for n-member groups where $n > 3$ we first need to meaningfully define the issue, as in such cases the concept of group performance is ambiguous. Do we compare the expert rule to the best alternative rule? Do we compare the performance of the expert rule to that of simple majority rule? Or maybe the performance of the most competent individual should be compared to the average performance of the relevant alternative rules? Computation of the optimality likelihoods for all relevant rules for any n-member group would certainly provide a satisfactory answer to the question. Unfortunately, at present, even the problem of identifying the relevant rules is not resolved, not to mention the obvious further difficulties associated with the development of a general algorithm capable of identifying the optimal relevant rule. For $n \leqslant 5$, however, the relevant weighted majority rules are known (see Table 2.1). In the next section we illustrate how the expert rule can be compared to all alternative relevant weighted majority rules assuming a five-member group and, again, a uniform distribution of decisional skills.

Table 5.3 *Estimated likelihood p^i for the optimality of the weighted majority rule defined by the weights w^i when $n = 5$ and p_i is uniformly distributed over $[0.5, 1]$.*

w_i	p_i
(1, 0, 0, 0, 0)	0.199
(1, 1, 1, 0, 0)	0.175
(2, 1, 1, 1, 0)	0.229
(1, 1, 1, 1, 1)	0.022
(3, 1, 1, 1, 1)	0.107
(2, 2, 1, 1, 1)	0.074
(3, 2, 2, 1, 1)	0.194

5.4 Optimality of all relevant rules in a five-member group under uniform distribution of competences

Consider a five-member group and with no loss of generality label the individuals such that $p_i \geqslant p_j$ for $i < j$. In this case there exist seven relevant weighted majority rules. The expert rule, simple majority rule and five other rules. The weights defining the expert rule are $(w_1, w_2, w_3, w_4, w_5) = (1, 0, 0, 0, 0)$. The weights defining simple majority rule are $(1, 1, 1, 1, 1)$. The weights defining the remaining relevant rules are $(1, 1, 1, 0, 0)$, $(2, 1, 1, 1, 0)$, $(2, 2, 1, 1, 1)$, $(3, 2, 2, 1, 1)$ and $(3, 1, 1, 1, 1)$. For a proof and further interpretation of these rules see Section 2.5 and the Appendix to Chapter 2.

Assuming that p_i is uniformly distributed between 0.5 and 1, we ran a Monte Carlo simulation generating 1000 five-member groups. Employing the optimality result mentioned in the opening paragraph of the preceding section we then determined for each group which of the seven rules is the optimal one. Table 5.3 displays the estimated likelihoods for the optimality of the seven relevant weighted majority rules.

The expert rule is likely to be the optimal rule with probability 0.199. Notice that the simulation reported in Table 5.2 generated an almost identical result. The rule most likely to be the optimal one is defined by the weights $(2, 1, 1, 1, 0)$. That is, according to this rule decisions are reached by applying the simple majority rule among the four more qualified individuals and, in cases of a tie, the collective decision becomes that of the most competent individual. Surprisingly, the simple majority rule is least likely to be the optimal rule and it is considerably inferior to the expert rule on a pairwise comparison. Also, note that dispensing of at least one individual (starting, of course, with the least competent) constitutes an optimal strategy for the group in $0.603 = (0.199 + 0.175 + 0.229)$ of the cases.

5.5   Complete ignorance and the superiority of simple majority rule in three-member groups

The preceding sections illustrate how the performance of the expert rule can be assessed under various particular partial information assumptions regarding individual decisional competences. Being able only to identify the expert (rather than to determine his exact decisional competence) is therefore a necessary condition for implementing the optimal group strategy in these partial information cases where the expert rule is indeed optimal. As we have seen, the optimality of the expert rule hinges upon our particular assumptions regarding group size and the form of the distribution of individual competences. Although partial information regarding competences might be available, the designer of the optimal decision rule for the group might even be unable to rank the group members by skill and, in particular, to identify the expert. In some cases even partial information is not available and attention is then focused on what, if anything, from our optimality analysis may be applied in such circumstances.

For the special case of three-member groups where $p_i \geq 0.5$ we propose that the expert rule is always the inferior rule provided that the selection of an 'expert' is interpreted as an even-chance lottery. Specifically, the selection of an individual as the expert is assumed to be equally likely to yield the most competent individual, the least competent individual and the median individual. Hence such a lottery guarantees the mean probability $\pi^e = \bar{p} = (p_1 + p_2 + p_3)/3$. On the other hand the alternative rule, simple majority rule, generates the probability $\pi^m = p_1 p_2 p_3 + p_1 p_2 (1 - p_3) + (1 - p_1) p_2 p_3 + p_1 (1 - p_2) p_3$. For any triple p_1, p_2, p_3, $\pi^m > \pi^e$ (see Proposition 3.5.4) and therefore simple majority rule is always preferable to the even-chance lottery taken by selecting the expert rule. To prove that $\pi^m > \pi^e$ note that

$$\pi^m(p_1, p_2, p_3) > \tfrac{1}{3}\pi^m(\tfrac{1}{2}, p_2, p_3) + \tfrac{1}{3}\pi^m(p_1, \tfrac{1}{2}, p_3) + \tfrac{1}{3}\pi^m(p_1, p_2, \tfrac{1}{2})$$

but

$$\pi^m(\tfrac{1}{2}, p_i p_j) = p_i p_j + \tfrac{1}{2}p_i(1 - p_j) + \tfrac{1}{2}p_j(1 - p_i)$$
$$= \tfrac{1}{2}(p_i + p_j)$$

So that the right-hand side of the above inequality is equal to

$$\tfrac{1}{3}[\tfrac{1}{2}(p_2 + p_3) + \tfrac{1}{2}(p_1 + p_3) + \tfrac{1}{2}(p_1 + p_2)] = \tfrac{1}{3}(p_1 + p_2 + p_3)$$
$$= \pi_{\bar{p}}$$
$$= \pi^e$$

CHAPTER 6

Interdependent decisions

6.1 Introduction

Individual decisional skills are rarely statistically independent. Numerous factors account at least for some degree of interdependence of individual competences in almost any conceivable decision-making group. Among the most pervasive factors are real or potential social pressures enhancing conformity, various forms of commitments, leadership effects, similar background or similar training of individuals, exchange of relevant information, threats, persuasion and, finally, false conceptions leading individuals to try and improve their group performance by adopting promising strategies such as following superior decision makers' views.

Some patterns of interaction among decision makers may positively affect individual skills in a manner analogous to that of a learning process. More generally, certain interactive processes may act as investment in human capital. In such cases the interaction among decision makers alters their vector of skills. That is, pursuant to the termination of the interaction process, the competency parameter of every individual reflects his past ability as well as his newly acquired capability.[1] Each individual's new decisional skill is totally unconditional upon any views of decisions of other individuals. This important form of interaction is not the subject of our discussion.

The analysis of all remaining special cases of interdependence is still a very tedious and possibly a hopelessly complex task. In relaxing the independence assumption we therefore further restrict our analysis to a special class of dependence patterns wherein the actual decisions of some members of N are dependent on the views or choices of some other group members, and the original decisional skills of each individual are maintained. Even in this case, however, we do not intend to cover all possible patterns of interaction. In particular, we disregard situations where decisions depend on the decision rule in use or on factors that are external to the model. Section 6.2 descrives the particular class of interdependence patterns on which this chapter focuses. If the independence condition is unlikely to be satisfied in most committees, panels of experts, juries, management boards, courts and other decision-making groups, then naturally one wonders what is the effect of inter-dependence on the optimal decision rules for the group N. In Section 6.3 we show that given our special class of dependence forms independent choices are always superior to dependent ones; the optimal group performance under independent decisions can only be adversely affected by any pattern of interaction belonging to our special class of interactions. For the special class of total interdependence forms, which is a widely observed form of inter-dependence, the optimal rule (again, a weighted majority rule) can be directly obtained using Theorem 2.3.1. Total interdependence means that every dependent individual totally belittles himself. Under such form of extreme self-denial the individual actual choices are dependent *only* on the views or decisions of others. The intuitive results of Section 6.3 imply that the main result of Chapter 2 (Theorem 2.3.1) retains its viability. If decisions are totally independent, then the optimal rule can be directly identified using Theorem 2.3.1. If decisions belong to our class of dependence patterns, without being necessarily total, then the optimal rule is not, in general, a weighted majority rule. However, in such a case any deviation from the independent pattern can only reduce the group performance. In other words, elimination of interdependence, if possible, will only serve a useful purpose from the group standpoint.

6.2   Interdependence

In order to formalize the notion of interdependence, let us partition the set of individuals N into two subsets I and D such that $I \cap D = \emptyset, I \cup D = N$. The set I consists of all individuals acting independently and the set D contains the remaining individuals. Note that $I \neq \emptyset$. Otherwise, a perpetual process is generated and group decision making becomes impossible. With no loss of generality, let $I = \{1, \ldots, m\}$ where $1 \leqslant m \leqslant n$. In turn, $D = \{m+1, \ldots, n\}$.

We let individual views prior to any interaction be represented by an n-tuple $z = (z_1, \ldots, z_n)$. Here $z_i = 1$ or -1 is interpreted as individual i's judgement supporting alternative a and alternative b respectively. The set of all possible views is $Z = \{1, -1\}^n = \{z = (z_1, \ldots, z_n): z_i \in \{1, -1\}, i = 1, \ldots, n\} = \Omega$. The actual vote of an independent decision maker coincides with his views. The relationship between a dependent individual's actual vote x_j and his and others' views is given by the function g_j where $g_j: (1, -1)^{m+1} \to (1, -1)$. That is, individual j's actual vote depends on his view as well as on the views of the independent members $i, \ldots m$. Furthermore, we require that the dependence scheme between j's actual vote and any relevant $(m+1)$-tuple of views be neutral. Specifically, if all relevant views change, so does individual j's vote, i.e. $g_j(-z_j, -z_1, \ldots, -z_m) = -g_j(z_j, z_1, \ldots, z_m)$ for any vector of views z in Z. In other words, although the independence assumption is relaxed, symmetry of the alternatives still holds and therefore neutrality of the values of g_i is required. A voting profile x is thus obtained from the vector of views z using the dependence transformation $g_{m+1}, \ldots, g_n$. Specifically, $\forall j \in I$, $x_j = z_j$, $\forall j \in D$, $x_j = g_i(z_j, z_1, \ldots, z_m)$. Denote by G the set $\{g_{m+1}, \ldots, g_n\}$. Thus, a dependence pattern is fully specified by D and G. Any dependence pattern is a transformation G from Ω to itself. The identity transformation is called the independence pattern and is denoted G_0. Under this latter pattern the set D is clearly empty.

Social pressure is often considered as the cause of an interdependence or as a deviation of G from G_0. Very often, such pressure is considered as a major force making for conformity. It is argued, for instance, that the desire to be an acceptable group member tends to silence actual disagreement and favors consensus. Majority opinions, according to the conventional wisdom, tend to be accepted. The following dependence pattern may serve as a typical example.

Let $D = \{n\}$, $I = \{1, \ldots, n-1\}$ and

$$
g_n(z_n, z_1, \ldots, z_{n-1}) = \begin{cases} \text{sign}\left(\sum_{i=1}^{n-1} z_i\right) & \text{if } \left|\sum_{i=1}^{n-1} z_i\right| > \alpha(n-1) \\ z_n & \text{otherwise} \end{cases}
$$

where $\frac{1}{2} < \alpha < 1$.

Here individual n is the only dependent decision maker. He follows the α-majority view when such a majority view exists. Otherwise he resorts to his own judgement; that is, he chooses according to his own view. Note that g_n is a neutral dependence function, i.e. $g_n(-Z_n, -z_1, \ldots, -z_{n-1}) = -g_n(z_n, z_1, \ldots, z_{n-1})$.

The decisional skill of any individual i is represented by the probability p_i that his view is correct. The probability of individual i actually making the correct choice depends, in general, on his decisional skill and on the specific dependence pattern G characterizing the interaction among decisions of members in N.

Returning to the above example, if $p_n \leqslant p_j$ for all $j \in I$, that is, if individual n is the least competent decision maker, then clearly his probability of voting correctly can be positively affected by the dependence pattern G. In other words, given G, $p_n \leqslant \Pr\{x_n \text{ is the correct choice}\}$. Individual n's dependence may be attributed to different factors within the realm of social psychology. It may also reflect n's belief that such dependence is a reasonable strategy to enable him, and in turn the group, to improve their performance. Such a belief might be induced by the seemingly desirable positive increment [$\Pr(x_n$ is the correct choice$\} - p_n$]. A dependence pattern that seems to be individually desirable may turn out to be spurious and, therefore, socially as well as individually undesirable. From the group standpoint, a key issue then is whether a particular interdependence pattern has a positive or a negative effect upon the probability of obtaining collectively the correct alternative. The analysis of this issue as well as some related problems constitute the main task of the following section.

6.3   Independent versus interdependent decision making

The probability of obtaining collectively the correct alternative now depends on three factors: first, the particular decision rule employed by the decision makers f; second, the skills of the decision makers $p = (p_1,\ldots,p_n)$; third, the interdependence pattern among the decision makers G. That is, $\pi = \pi(f,p,G)$. The following result establishes in a simple but rigorous manner the intuitive tenet that interaction between decision makers is often dysfunctional. In our model any interdependence pattern G cannot be superior to the independence pattern G_0. We state this formally in the following theorem.

Theorem 6.3.1 Let $\hat{f}$ be the optimal rule under independent decisions; that is, $\pi(\hat{f},p,G_0) \geqslant \pi(f,p,G_0)$ for any neutral f and any given skills vector p. Then, for any neutral interdependence pattern G and any decisive decision rule f

$$\pi(\hat{f},\, p,\, G_0) \geqslant \pi(f,\, p,\, G)$$

Proof: Given a neutral rule f and an interdependence scheme G, define a rule h, $h: Z \rightarrow (1, -1)$ using the pair f, G

$$h(z_1,\ldots,z_n|\, f,\, G)$$

$$\equiv f(z_1,\ldots,z_m,\, g_{m+1})(z_{m+1},\, z_1,\ldots,z_m),\ldots,g_n(z_n,z_1,\ldots,z_m)$$

By assumption, f is neutral and g_j, $j = m+1,\ldots,n$, are neutral. Hence, h is neutral. Under the interdependence pattern G_0, the range of h is Ω. Clearly, then, $\pi(h,p,G_0) = \pi(f,p,G)$. By assumption, $\pi(\hat{f},p,G_0) \geqslant \pi(f,p,G_0)$ for any neutral f. In particular, $\pi(\hat{f},p,G_0) \geqslant \pi(h,p,G_0)$ and therefore, $\pi(\hat{f},p,G_0) \geqslant \pi(f,p,G)$.

Usually, the vector of decisional competences p and the dependence pattern G are both externally given. For any pair (p, G) there exists an optimal rule f^0. That is, the rule f^0 secures the largest probability of obtaining the correct decision given both individual abilities and the particular pattern of interdependence among their choices.

The above result implies that, given independent decision making, the optimal rule cannot be inferior to the optimal rule corresponding to any pattern of interdependence, provided that individual skills are held constant. This implies that any form of interdependence has an effect on the performance of the group N similar to the introduction of an additional constraint into the problem

$$\max_{f} \pi(f,\, p,\, G_0)$$

Our theorem does not provide a constructive solution to the problem the group faces under the common situations where p and G are given. Put differently, although we do know $\hat{f}$ we cannot generally construct f^0. It does suggest, however, that whenever the pattern of interaction G is a control variable, the designer of the optimal decision rule should better transform it into G_0. In other words, any dependence structure within the class of structures on which this monograph focuses can only adversely affect the performance of the group. Such an effect is due to the disposition of some useful decisional resources associated with any harmful pattern of interdependence.

A second immediate implication of the above theorem suggests that the employment of the optimal decision rule $\hat{f}$, given independent voting, is superior, in fact weakly superior, to using the same rule when decisions are interrelated by a pattern G, $G \neq G_0$. The following obvious corollary summarizes the above applications.

Corollary 6.3.1 (1) For a given vector of skills p and interdependence pattern G let f^0 be a decisive decision rule satisfying $\pi(f^0, p, G) \geqslant \pi(f, p, G)$ for any neutral f. Then

    (i) $\pi(\hat{f}, p, G_0) \geqslant \pi(f^0, p, G)$

    (ii) $\pi(\hat{f}, p, G_0) \geqslant \pi(\hat{f}, p, G)$

Corollary 6.3.1 (1) bears significant consequences for situations where the dependence pattern among individual decisions is a decision variable. For such situations the more independent the group members are the better.[2] A possible way of adhering to such a recommendation is by augmenting the optimal decision-making rule with appropriate institutions or procedures designed to maintain the independence of the decision-making process. A clear example of such a procedure is secret voting.

The traditional argument in favor of secret voting typically runs as follows: A voter can be held to account only if his vote is known; therefore, without open voting, corruption or intimidation by a few powerful decision makers or by the pressure of public opinion cannot exist. More generally, with open voting, the collective decision-making process is more vulnerable to manipulation of various sorts and, in turn, to voters' preference misrepresentation.

The case against secret voting is not so obvious and is now of interest largely because it was forcibly put forward by J.S. Mill in his advocacy of representative government. His arguments, which still have some relevance to the experience of compact social groups, emphasize the possibility that secret voting may hinder a kind of responsible democratic process, that of reaching general agreement by open discussion (Mill, 1861). In our context, voters, members of professional committees, experts, managers or judges have no conflict of interest, and by assumption, decisional skills are held fixed. In other words, members of N are unanimously agreed upon ends but there is a possible conflict over means (alternative a or alternative b). Here the traditional arguments for or against secret voting are irrelevant. The issue of open versus secret voting remains, however, of considerable significance and given our stylized decision theory model, it can be formally approached, analyzed and resolved by resorting to straightforward efficiency considerations. Specifically, we can simply compare the effects of the two possible procedures on the objective function π.

Corollary 6.3.1 (1) unequivocally resolves the dilemma, provided that one accepts the tenable presumption that secret voting guarantees a greater degree of independence among individual decisions. To facilitate exposition, consider the extreme case where secret voting is associated with G_0 and open voting is associated with some G, $G \neq G_0$. If the group N operates optimally under open voting, then by (i) of Corollary 6.3.1 (1) it can be concluded that the replacement of the open voting procedure with secret voting might be beneficial to the group. If the group N operates optimally under secret voting, then using (ii) of Corollary 6.3.1 (1), it can be concluded that replacing secret voting with open voting can only be harmful to the collective interest. Within our framework, secret voting thus emerges as the desirable mode of voting, given that the group indeed designs the optimal decision-making apparatus. If the decision rule that the group adopts under secret voting differs from $\hat{f}$, then it is perfectly possible that open voting improves the collective judgement. Put differently, if for some reason the group is restricted in choosing among decision rules (a not untenable assumption when the model is enriched to include, for example, cost considerations, as in Chapter 2), then the formation of dependence patterns might be advantageous, serving as a vehicle to bypass institutional, organizational, technological or economic constraints inhibiting the selection of certain rules, in particular, the rule $\hat{f}$. Under such circumstances the issue of open versus secret voting cannot be a priori resolved without information on p, G and the constrained subset of feasible decision rules the group confronts.

Example 6.3.1 $N = \{1, 2, 3\}$, $p = (p_1, p_2, p_3)$, $p_1 \geqslant p_2 \geqslant p_3$. Suppose that G_0 is associated with secret voting, and G is associated with open voting, such that $I = \{1\}$, $D = \{2, 3\}$, $g_2(z_2, z_1) = z_1, g_3(z_3, z_1) = z_1$. For a three-member decision-making body there exist two relevant neutral decision rules (see Table 2.1). The expert rule $f_1(x_1, x_2, x_3) = x_1$ and simple majority rule $f_2(x_1, x_2, x_3) = \text{sign} (x_1 + x_2 + x_3)$. Suppose that the group N is restricted to using f_2. If N operates under secret voting, then

$$\pi(f_2, p, G_0) = p_1 p_2 p_3 + p_1 p_2 (1 - p_3) + p_1 (1 - p_2) p_3 + (1 - p_1) p_2 p_3$$

If N operates under open voting, then $\pi(f_2, p, G) = p_1$. It can be readily verified that if

$$\frac{p_1}{1 - p_1} > \frac{p_2}{(1 - p_2)} \frac{p_3}{(1 - p_3)}, \quad \text{then } \pi(f_2, p, G) > \pi(f_2, p, G_0)$$

This illustrates the possible superiority of open voting when the group cannot select the unconstrained optimal rule $\hat{f}$. (In our case $\hat{f}$ is the expert rule f_1. Obviously, $\pi(f_1, p, G_0) = p_1$.)

In the above example, both individual 2 and individual 3 demonstrate an extreme mode of self-denial. Such total dependence is quite commonly observed under various circumstances where the impact of leaders, the effect of collegiality or the degree of individual insecurity is extreme. A general definition of total interdependence is presented below.

An interdependence pattern G is called *total* whenever the members of D never resort to their own judgement in making an actual decision, i.e. $g_j(z_j, z_1, \ldots, z_m) \equiv g_j(z_1, \ldots, z_m)$ for every $j = m + 1, \ldots, n$. A particular case of total interdependence occurs when a single leader is blindly followed by all other decision makers, as in the previous example. Less extreme cases are characterized by a more balanced collegiality pattern. For example, the dependent individuals may follow the majority view held by a recognized subset of qualified decision makers (the experts). The more common cases are, of course, those where different subsets of dependent individuals are inspired by their particular subsets of independent individuals. For example, several independent individuals may be supported by their totally dependent factions. For total interdependence patterns we can add the following constructive corollary.

Corollary 6.3.1 (2) Let G be a total interdependence pattern with $I = \{1, \ldots, m\}$. Then, for a given vector of skills p, $\pi(f^0, p, G) \geq (f, p, G)$ for any neutral f, if

$$f^0(x_1, \ldots, x_n) = \text{sign} \left(\sum_{i=1}^{m} \beta_i x_i \right)$$

where $\beta_i = \ln (p_i/(1 - p_i))$.

Proof : If G is total, then

$$\pi(f,\, p,\, G) = \pi(f,\, (p_1,\ldots,p_n),\, G)$$
$$= \pi(f,\, (p_1,\ldots,p_m),\, G_0)$$

That is, the probability of choosing correctly given f, $(p_1,\ldots,p_n)$ and G is identical to the probability of obtaining a correct choice in the group $I = \{1,\ldots,m\}$ given f, $(p_1,\ldots,p_m)$ and G_0. By Theorem 2.3.1, the optimal rule is indeed f^0.

Corollary 6.3.1 (2) emphasizes that the nature of the optimality result under independent voting is unaltered when the interdependence pattern is total. In these latter cases the dependent members of N should become inessential and the independent members are assigned the same weights as under the rule $\hat{f}$.

Our concluding example illustrates the two corollaries of the main result. It also demonstrates the viability of the two corollaries presenting a situation where $\pi(\hat{f}, p, G_0) > \pi(f^0, p, G) > \pi(\hat{f}, p, G).$[3]

Example 6.3.2

$N = \{1, 2, 3, 4\}$

$p = (p_1, p_2, p_3, p_4)$ where
$$\begin{cases} p_1 \geqslant p_2 \geqslant p_3 \geqslant p_4 \geqslant \quad \text{and} \\[2mm] \dfrac{p_1}{(1-p_1)} < \dfrac{p_2}{(1-p_2)}\dfrac{p_3}{(1-p_3)} < \dfrac{p_1}{(1-p_1)}\dfrac{p_4}{(1-p_4)} \end{cases}$$

In a four-member group there exist only three relevant neutral decision rules (see Table 2.1): the expert rule, f_1; the simple majority rule applied among the three most competent individuals f_2; and the simple majority rule with a tie-breaking chairman f_3 (the most qualified individual being the chairman). Given our assumption on the vector p

$$\pi(f_3,\, p,\, G_0) > \pi(f_2,\, p,\, G_0) > \pi(f_1,\, p,\, G_0)$$

(see Section 3.4). Now consider the total interdependence scheme G where $D = \{4\}$, $I = \{1,2,3\}$ and $g_4(z_4, z_1, z_2, z_3) = z_1$. By Corollary 6.3.1 (2), $f^0(p, G) = f_2$ and hence $\pi(f^0, p, G) = \pi(f_2, p, G)$. By Theorem 2.3.1, $\hat{f}(p, G_0) = f_3$, and therefore $\pi(\hat{f}, p, G_0) = \pi(f_3, p, G_0)$. By definition of G, $\pi(f_3, p, G) = \pi(f_1, p, G_0)$. We thus obtain, $\pi(\hat{f}, p, G_0) > \pi(f^0, p, G) > \pi(\hat{f}, p, G)$.

CHAPTER 7

Improving decisional skills as investment in human capital

7.1   Introduction

Most studies of investment in human capital including Becker (1964), Ben-Porath (1967) and Mincer (1974) measure the rate of return on such investment by the increment to the individual's future income. Although several writers in the field of labor economics note the difference between the individual and social rates of return on investment in human capital, most analytical models disregard it; consequently the social rate of return has not received the treatment it deserves.

This chapter presents a variant of our stylized model which is primarily designed to analyze social investment decisions in human capital.[1] In this model the sole motive for investment in human capital is the attempt to reduce the probability of making incorrect decisions. More specifically, in an uncertain environment the individual decision maker is always liable to make a wrong decision; but the greater the investment in human capital, the smaller the probability of error. In fact, in such a model investment in human capital plays the same role as a hedge against risk in the form of 'self-protection'.[2] Such activity will raise the individual's expected income or, more generally, his expected benefit, not directly by increasing the amount of income but by increasing his likelihood of making correct decisions and, in turn, by benefiting from them.

On the social level, the element of self-protection means that it is in the public interest to invest in members of the society. Members of society are represented by a common production function which relates amount of investment to their decisional skills. Investment in members of society stems from the attempt to increase the net social expected benefit associated with the decisions that society undertakes. Such an objective can be realized by reducing the probability of individual (and, by extension, collective) incorrect decisions. The social rate of return to such an investment is the increase in the net social expected benefit and it is obtained through the increase in the likelihood of society making the correct decisions using a given collective decision-making process. In the present context, this process is assumed to be the commonly used majority rule.

In the following section we start with the individual's investment problem. Section 7.3 contains the analysis of the social human capital allocation problem for a fixed number of homogeneous decision makers. It is shown that an optimal investment schedule in human capital implies equal investment in each individual. The necessary conditions for an internal solution (a positive per capita investment) to the social allocation problem is a sufficiently large net gain to be associated with the social decisions (Proposition 7.3.1). Comparative statics reveal, first, that a larger net gain justifies a more intensive investment in human capital and, second, that the larger the size of society the smaller the optimum per capita investment in human capital (Proposition 7.3.2). The relationship between the optimum expected net social benefit and group size is then partly established in Proposition 7.3.3. This chapter concludes with a comparison of the democratic system and its 'decentralized equivalent', both in terms of their efficiency and in terms of the total volume of investment they induce. A decision system based on majority rule is always more efficient than its decentralized equivalent. The relationship between total social investment in human capital under the two systems is established in Proposition 7.3.4. We show that if individual ability in the democratic system is sufficiently large, then total investment in human capital in this system is less than in the decentralized system.

7.2   The individual decision-maker's problem

Consider an individual who has to choose between the two mutually exclusive alternatives: 'correct' and 'incorrect'. We assume that the ability of the decision maker can be parameterized by a single number p which represents his objective, personal probability of making the correct choice. The expected gain from this choice is

$$e = pb_s + (1 - p)b_f$$

where b_s is the benefit resulting from a correct decision, and b_f is the benefit (or cost) if he fails to choose correctly. Obviously $b_s > b_f$.

Suppose now that p is not entirely exogenous to the decision maker but can be increased through investment in human capital. Such an investment, in terms of money or time, can take several forms such as schooling, on-the-job training, health care, social interaction in a study group and search for information (see for instance Paroush and Peles (1978) and Paroush (1981)). Denote by h the amount invested in human capital,[3] and let $C(h)$ be the cost of such an investment. We assume that

$$p'(h) > 0$$
$$\tfrac{1}{2} < p(h) < 1 \quad \text{for } 0 \leqslant h < \infty$$
$$C'(h) > 0$$
$$p''(h) \leqslant 0$$
$$C''(h) \geqslant 0$$

and that at least one of the last two inequalities is strict.

The individual's objective is to maximize his expected net benefit, or equivalently, since b_s is constant,

$$(7.2.1) \quad \max_h \{p(h)b - C(h)\} \quad \text{where } b = b_s - b_f$$

The investment h^0 is the solution to this problem. The first-order condition for a regular internal solution is

$$(7.2.2) \quad p'(h)b = C'(h)$$

Given our assumptions regarding $p''(h)$ and $C''(h)$, the second-order condition

$$p''(h)b < C''(h)$$

is always satisfied. Since at the optimal solution h^0, $p'(h^0) > 0$ and $p''(h^0)b - C''(h^0) < 0$, comparative statics with respect to b reveals that

$$\frac{dh^0}{db} = -\frac{p'(h^0)}{[p''(h^0)b - C''(h^0)]} > 0$$

which means that the higher the net gain of a correct decision, the larger the amount invested in human capital.

7.3   The collective decision-making problem

7.3.1 *A homogeneous society of fixed size*

Consider a group of $2k + 1$ individuals – a board of managers, a professional panel, a jury, or society as a whole – with identical potential ability (all sharing the same ability production function $p(h)$) and tastes, who wish to choose between the two alternatives: 'correct' and 'incorrect'. We assume that collective decisions are obtained by the widely-used majority rule, where the group votes on the two alternatives and selects the one that receives more votes (abstentions are not allowed). If $p(h_i)$ represents individual i's probability of making a correct decision, then the probability $\hat{\pi}$ of arriving at a correct decision under majority rule with $2k + 1$ participants is the sum of all

$$\binom{2k + 1}{j} = \frac{(2k + 1)!}{j!(2k + 1 - j)!}$$

products of j of the $p(h_i)$ and $2k + 1 - j$ of the terms $[1 - p(h_i)]$ with each i appearing exactly once in each product and the sum being over j ($j = k + 1, \ldots, 2k + 1$).

When the number of participants in the social decision process is fixed (k is fixed), the optimum investment schedule in human capital $(h_1, \ldots, h_{2k+1})$ is obtained by solving

(7.3.1) $\max\limits_{h_1, \ldots, h_{2k+1}} V(h_1, \ldots, h_{2k+1})$

where $V(h_1, \ldots, h_{2k+1}) = \hat{\pi}[p(h_1), \ldots, p(h_{2k+1}); k]B - \hat{C}(h_1, \ldots, h_{2k+1}; k)$. B is the net social benefit of a correct decision $B = B_s - B_f$, and $\hat{C}(h_1, \ldots, h_{2k+1}; k)$ is the social cost of investment in human capital. Again, we assume $p'(h_i) > 0$, $p''(h_i) \leq 0$, $\partial C/\partial h_i > 0$, $\partial^2 C/\partial h_i^2 \geq 0$.

Suppose that $\hat{C}$ is symmetric in its $2k + 1$ arguments, then V is also a symmetric function because $\hat{\pi}$ is symmetric. In such a case the optimal investment in human capital necessarily implies an equal investment in each individual, i.e. $h_i = h$ for every $i = 1, 2, \ldots, 2k + 1$. This statement may be supported by the following reasoning: the function V is assumed to be strictly concave and, therefore, it has a unique solution. However, if the optimum solution differs from $h_i = h$, then we must have at least $2k$ additional solutions because of the symmetry of V, which is in contradiction to the uniqueness.

Thus, problem (7.3.1) can be reduced to a maximization problem of a single variable

(7.3.2) $\max\limits_{h} V(h)$

where $V(h) = \pi[p(h); k]B - C(h; k)$, $C(h; k) = \hat{C}(h, h, \ldots, h; k)$ and

$$\pi(p(h); k) = \sum_{i=k+1}^{2k+1} \binom{2k + 1}{i} p(h)^i [1 - p(h)]^{2k+1-i}$$
$$= \hat{\pi}[p(h), \ldots, p(h); k]$$

The first-order condition for a regular internal solution of (7.3.2) is

(7.3.3) $Bp'(h)\dfrac{\partial \pi}{\partial p} - C'(h) = 0$

The second-order condition is

$$\Delta = \left[p''(h)\frac{\partial \pi}{\partial p} + (p'(h))^2 \frac{\partial^2 \pi}{\partial p^2} \right] B - \frac{\partial^2 C}{\partial h^2} < 0$$

Since

$$\frac{\partial \pi}{\partial p} = (2k+1)\binom{2k}{k}\{p(1-p)\}^k > 0$$

and

$$\frac{\partial^2 \pi}{\partial p^2} = (2k+1)k\binom{2k}{k}\{p(1-p)\}^{k-1}(1-2p) < 0$$

for every $\frac{1}{2} < p < 1$, the second-order condition holds for every h, and once again

$$\frac{dh}{dB} = -p'(h)\frac{\partial \pi}{\partial p}\bigg/ \Delta > 0$$

Therefore, the two simple problems presented (the individual's as well as that of the homogeneous society) imply the accepted and easily observable phenomenon that the higher the net gain from decisions, the larger the optimum amount of investment in human capital.

To stress this last point further, assume that the cost function $\hat{C}$ has two components; the cost of investment in human capital

$$\sum_{i=1}^{n} h_i$$

where h_i is the amount invested in member i, and the decision-making costs $c(2k+1)$ which are proportional to the size of the group.

If so, then

$$C(h, k) = (h+c)(2k+1)$$

Under this special, but quite general form of the cost function it pays to invest in human capital ($h^* > 0$) only if B is sufficiently large. More precisely, there is always a critical value B_0 such that society will invest in human capital, as a measure of self-protection, only if the net benefit exceeds B_0.

Proposition 7.3.1[4] Denote by h_k^* the solution of (7.3.2). Then

$$h_k^* \begin{cases} = 0 & \text{if } B \leqslant B_0 \\ > 0 & \text{if } B > B_0 \end{cases}$$

where

(7.3.3) $$\frac{1}{B_0} = \binom{2k}{k}p'(0)\{p(0)[1-p(0)]\}^k$$

This proposition states that the critical value is determined by three factors: first, the initial skill of the homogeneous decision makers, i.e. the endowed probability of making a correct decision with no investment in human capital $p(0)$; second, the rate of return, in probability terms, to such an investment at the initial point $p'(0)$; and third, the size of society k. By (7.3.3) we can observe that B_0 is inversely related to $p'(0)$ and, at the extreme case where $p'(0)$ is infinitely high, a positive investment in human capital should always be made.

Since, by assumption, $\frac{1}{2} < p(0) < 1$, (7.3.3) implies that B_0 is a monotone increasing function of $p(0)$. Thus, the incentive to invest in human capital is stronger the lower the initial skill of the decision makers. If $p(0)$ is close to unity, there is no need to invest in human capital because society is already sufficiently protected unless, of course, the net social benefit B is extremely high. Finally, it is not difficult to verify by (7.3.3) that B_0 is also a monotone increasing function of k. Moreover, B_0 tends to infinity with k, so that, if the decision group is large enough, there is no need for investment in human capital regardless of the size of the net benefit B; in this sense, the size of the set of decision makers is a perfect substitute for self-protection. The direct relation between B_0 and k, which is a corollary of Proposition 7.3.1, establishes the positive relation between self-protection and the size of society in qualitative terms. Such a relation can be further and quantitatively substantiated by showing that the optimum amount invested in human capital h^* is a monotone decreasing function of society size k.

Proposition 7.3.2 Denote by h_k^* the solution of

$$\max_h V(h;k)$$

then

$$h_r^* \leqslant h_k^*, \quad \text{for every } r > k$$

That is, investment in human capital is inversely related to the number of individuals participating in the collective decision-making process. The larger the size of society the smaller the optimum per capita investment in human capital.

Finally, we examine the sensitivity of the optimum value of the objective function $V(h_k^*;k) = V^*(k)$ to variations in k. Consider first the case where $h_k^* = 0$.[5] Here

$$V^*(k) = B\pi(p(0);k) - c(2k + 1)$$
$$dV^*(k) = V^*(k + 1) - V^*(k) = Bd\pi - 2c$$
$$d\pi = \pi(p(0); k + 1) - \pi(p(0); k)$$

Proposition 7.3.3 Suppose $h_k^* = 0$. Then there exists k_0 such that

$$dV^* \begin{cases} > 0 & \text{for } k < k_0 \\ < 0 & \text{for } k > k_0 \end{cases}$$

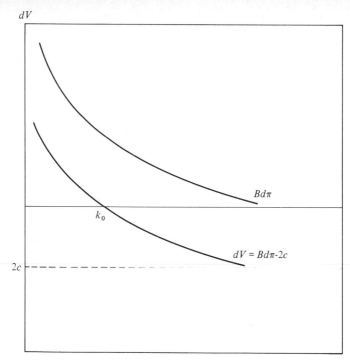

Figure 7.1. The sensitivity of optimal expected net benefit to variations in $k - dV^*(k)$.

That is, the expected net benefit $V(k)$ increases with k up to a certain group size (k_0) and thereafter declines (see Figure 7.1). If $c = 0$, then $k_0 = \infty$. In this case the expected net benefit tends to B because

$$\lim_{k \to \infty} \pi = 1$$

and there are no costs to enlarging the size of the decision-making body.[6] If $p(0) = \frac{1}{2}$, then $V^*(k) = B/2 - c(2k + 1)$, and thus the largest expected net benefit is obtained when the size of the group is minimized.

When $h_k^* > 0$, the relationship between $V^*(k)$ and the size of the group is ambiguous. Additional assumptions on the skill production function $p(h)$ are clearly needed in order to eliminate this ambiguity.

We now turn to the comparison between the total volume of investment in human capital under the decentralized system, where each individual solves problem (7.2.1) and its volume under the democratic system in which the social problem is given by (7.3.2).

7.3.2 *The volume of investment under the centralized system versus the decentralized equivalent system*

In a decentralized decision system each of the society's $2k + 1$ individuals is assumed to solve problem (7.2.1) independently. In analogy to the social cost function $C(h, k)$, let the individual's cost function be given by $C(h) = c + h$, and denote the individual's optimal investment in human capital by h^0.

In the democratic multiperson public-choice model the social problem is given by (7.3.2). Here, $C(h, k) = (2k + 1)(c + h)$ and B, the net gain from the collective decision, is assumed to be the sum of the individual net gains, i.e. $B = (2k + 1)b$. The optimal per capita investment in human capital in this case is h^*. The important question to be considered now is under which system will total investment in human capital be larger? In particular, is it true that larger investments will always be made in the centralized system because of the positive difference between the social and the private rates of return?

Notice that under our assumptions a collective decision based on simple majority rule is always preferable to the outcome produced in a decentralized system. However, the amount invested in human capital in the former system is not necessarily larger. More specifically, there is some value $\frac{1}{2} < \bar{p} < 1$ such that only if $p(h^*) < \bar{p}$ will the centralized system invest more in human capital, as a means of self-protection, than its decentralized equivalent.

Proposition 7.3.4 $h^0 \gtreqless h^*$ if $p(h^*) \lesseqgtr \bar{p}$, where $\bar{p}$ solves the equation

$$\frac{\partial \pi}{\partial p} - 1 = 0$$

For example, when $k = 1$, $\pi = p^3 + 3p^2(1 - p)$ and $\partial \pi / \partial p = 6p(1 - p)$. In turn, $\bar{p} = 0.7866$, as illustrated in Figure 7.2. Consequently, if the common ability in a democratic decision-making system is smaller (greater) than 0.7866, then the implied total investment in human capital is larger (smaller) than the total investment in a decentralized system. The two systems yield an identical total investment in human capital when $p(h_k^*) = 0.7866$. As k increases, the magnitude of the critical ability will decrease (see Figure 7.2). Hence, if the ability of a representative individual in a democratic system is sufficiently large, then total investment is necessarily smaller than that in the decentralized equivalent system.

Throughout this chapter we assume that group decisions are obtained by the commonly-used majority rule. The analysis could be pursued assuming other collective decision-making processes. Moreover, the social decision procedure could be treated as in other chapters as a decision variable which, of course, considerably generalizes the optimization problem treated (problem 7.3.1). Also, in our model, both the potential and the initial ability of all

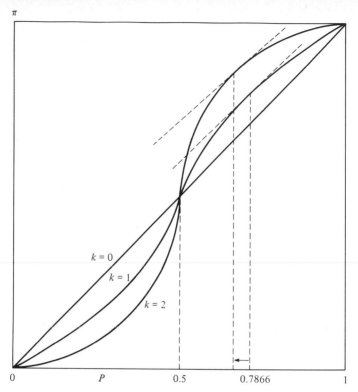

Figure 7.2. The probability of correct decision under simple majority rule
with $2k + 1$ identical decision makers $\pi(p; k)$; $k = 0, 1, 2$.

individuals is equal, i.e. $p_i(h) = p_j(h)$ for every two individuals i and j. Usually,
individual initial abilities can differ, that is, $p(h_i) \neq p(h_j)$. More generally,
potential abilities may also differ, that is, different individuals can be
characterized by different skill production functions: $p_i(h) \neq p_j(h)$. A more
complete treatment of the social investment problem in human capital should
clearly take both of these generalizations into account.

Appendix

Proposition 7.3.1 Denote by h_k^* the solution of (7.3.2), then

$$h_k^* \begin{cases} = 0 & \text{if } B \leqslant B_0 \\ > 0 & \text{if } B > B_0 \end{cases}$$

where

$$\frac{1}{B_0} = \binom{2k}{k} p'(0)\{p(0)[1 - p(0)]\}^k$$

Proof: Substitute $C'(h) = 2k + 1$ and

$$\partial\pi/\partial p = (2k + 1)\binom{2k}{k}\{p(1 - p)\}^k$$

in (7.3.3) to find that h_k^* satisfies the equation

(1) $$Bp'(h)\binom{2k}{k}\{p(h)[1 - p(h)]\}^k = 1$$

By assumption, $p(h)$ is bounded, $p''(h) < 0$ for every h and therefore

$$\lim_{h \to \infty} p'(h) = 0$$

Since $\frac{1}{2} < p < 1$, $p(h)[1 - p(h)]$ is a decreasing function of h. Consequently, (1) has a unique solution $h_k^* > 0$ unless

$$Bp'(0)\binom{2k}{k}\{p(0)[1 - p(0)]\}^k < 1$$

in which case $h_k^* = 0$.

Proposition 7.3.2 Denote by h_k^* the solution of (7.3.2), then

$$h_r^* \leqslant h_k^* \quad \text{for every } r > k$$

Proof: First note that by proposition 1 if $h_k^* = 0$, then $h_r^* = 0$ for every $r > k$. If $h_k^* > 0$, it solves equation (1) but the LHS of (1) is a decreasing function of h for any given k and a decreasing function of k for any given value of h, which completes the proof.

Proposition 7.3.3 If $h_k^* = 0$ then there exists k_0 such that

$$dV^* = Bd\pi - 2c \begin{cases} < 0 & k < k_0 \\ > 0 & k > k_0 \end{cases}$$

where

$$d\pi = \pi(p(0), k + 1) - \pi(p(0), k)$$

Proof: By calculation we can find that for $p(0) > \frac{1}{2}$

$$d\pi = \binom{2k + 1}{k + 1} p^{k+1}(1 - p)^{k+1}(2p - 1) > 0$$

and

$$d^2\pi = d\pi \left[4p(1-p) - 1 - \frac{2p(1-p)}{k+2} \right] < 0$$

which completes the proof.

Proposition 7.3.4 $h^0 \gtreqless h^*$ if $p(h^*) \lesseqgtr \bar{p}$ where $\bar{p}$ solves the equation

$$\frac{\partial \pi}{\partial p} - 1 = 0$$

Proof: If $C(h) = c + h$ then, by (7.2.2), h^0 satisfies $p'(h) = b^{-1}$ and, by (7.3.3), h^* satisfies $p'(h)\, \partial\pi/\partial p = b^{-1}$.

Therefore,

$$\frac{p'(h^0) - p'(h^*)}{p'(h^*)} = \frac{\partial \pi}{\partial p} - 1$$

Since $p'' < 0$, the proof is completed.

CHAPTER 8

Sequential analysis: the consulting case

8.1   Introduction

In the preceding chapters the size of the decision group is considered as a deterministic factor. This factor appears in the objective function of the group either as a fixed parameter (e.g. Chapter 2) or as a control variable (Chapter 3). In the current chapter the group size n is viewed as a random variable. More specifically, in Chapter 2 a collective decision rule is defined as a function f, such that for any decision profile x, $f(x) \in \{1, -1\}$. Here we are concerned with a decisive decision process which is a sequence of functions f_k, such that $f_k(x_1, \ldots, x_k) \in \{1, -1, A\}$ where 1 indicates a collective selection of alternative a, -1 indicates the selection of alternative b and A indicates adding another element to the decision profile $(x_1, \ldots, x_k)$. In other words, making another observation on the actual decision of individual $k+1$ is a third available option for the group. At any stage, except the last one, the group decision is no longer decisive with respect to the only two available alternatives, since the continuation of the decision process from stage k, with a decision profile $(x_1, \ldots, x_k)$, to stage $k+1$, where the decision profile is $(x_1, \ldots, x_k, x_{k+1})$, is a permissible outcome for the collective decision process. The sequential decision process f_k generalizes the concept of a decisive decision rule f, and the analysis of the corresponding extended version of the basic model constitutes the main purpose of this chapter. We pursue the sequential analysis using the interpretation suggested in the consulting example of Section 3.3. Such a restriction of context is deliberately chosen here because the consulting context offers the most significant economic application of the current extended version of our basic model.

The pioneering work of Stigler (1961) on the economics of information has stimulated a large amount of research in several fields, such as labor economics and investment in human capital; portfolio selection analysis and financial markets; demand and market research, to mention just a few (see, for instance,

McCall (1970), Mortenson (1970), Paroush (1974), Paroush and Peles (1978) and Paroush (1981)). Some of these works analyze sequential decision procedures while others concentrate on policies of the once-and-for-all type. Consulting is, in a sense, another special case within the field of economics of information.

A consultation is an action that one undertakes when faced with a dilemma or a choice situation. Usually, consulting is considered as a process of gathering of data and information in order to improve the consultor's skill in selecting the optimal alternative from a set of alternatives, or in order to increase the likelihood of making a correct decision in an uncertain environment. As such, consulting has all the characteristics of an investment which, on the one hand, provides some return and, on the other, involves certain costs. Obviously, there emerges the problem of what is the optimal amount of investment. More specifically, the individual faces the question of which stopping rule to use in his consulting process. For instance, an individual who faces the dilemma of whether or not to undergo radical surgery may in this connection be concerned with the question of how many physicians he should consult before taking a final decision.

This chapter addresses itself to such problems with the purpose of characterizing the optimal solution. Note that there is one aspect which distinguishes consulting from other kinds of investment in human capital. Investment in most cases depreciates with time, while the information gathered in a consulting process is used, in most cases, at one moment only, when the decision is taken.

Section 8.2 presents a model of individuals' behavior within which the problem of optimal quantity demanded of consulting services is posed and solved. The optimal stopping rules are derived. For simplicity, a highly stylized model is presented but we believe that the analysis sheds light on more general situations and that some of the results might also be applied to problems which are closer to reality. As in other cases, sequential techniques are more efficient in terms of expected benefit but possibly, as shall be seen, at the expense of a higher risk and therefore the sequential procedures are not always preferred.

8.2   The model, the problem and the solution

Consider an individual facing a set of two alternatives, say a and b, from which one and only one is optimal with respect to the individual's preferences. Assume that the individual knows how to distinguish between the two alternatives, say by name or by label, but because of lack of information or lack of skill or for reasons of uncertainty, he does not know how to identify which of the two is optimal for him. Moreover, assume that the decision maker does not assign any prior probabilities to the alternatives so that, from his viewpoint, the problem which he faces is entirely symmetrical, i.e. the problem is invariant under relabelling the alternatives. Obviously, under such circumstances, if compelled to choose without the help of any consulting service, our individual would take a fifty-fifty chance and pick at random one of the two alternatives as his choice. However, if the probability of a half to choose wrongly is too high for him (being for instance risk-averse) a demand for consulting services is generated. The quantity of consulting services demanded by the individual essentially depends on two factors: the cost (direct and indirect) for such a service and the amount of risk which the individual is willing to bear.

A consultant, as distinct from the individual, is supposed to be equipped with some expertise for identifying the optimal alternative. Assume that this expertise can be parameterized by a single number p which is the probability of choosing the optimal alternative and, again, p is assumed to be larger than a half. Moreover, assume that there is an unlimited number of consultants who possess exactly the same level of expertise p.

This assumption of consultants' homogeneous skill is relaxed later on. The consultants are assumed to provide their services independently so that the consulting process is entirely analogous to experimenting with independent Bernoulli trials (see Feller (1968, p. 135)). Denote the advice of consultant i by a random variable X_i which takes the value 1 if alternative a is recommended as optimal and the value 0 if alternative b is recommended as optimal. Formally

$$\Pr\{X_i = 1 \text{ given that } a \text{ is optimal}\} = p$$
$$\Pr\{X_i = 1 \text{ given that } b \text{ is optimal}\} = 1 - p$$

Note that the possibility of abstention is excluded. The individual's problem can be formulated and solved in two different versions: a non-sequential version analogous to that treated in Section 3.2 and a sequential version. We shall start with the first one.

8.2.1 The non-sequential version

In this case the individual's problem is to find a non-sequential decision process d and a number of consultants n (amount of consulting services) so that the expected net benefit is maximized, i.e.

$$(8.2.1) \quad \max_{d,n} \left[B\pi(n, d; p) - C(n, d; p) \right]$$

where $B > 0$ is the net benefit of a correct decision, π is the probability of a correct decision and C is the total cost involved. It is most likely that for any given d both π and C are non-decreasing functions of n and p. Also, as in

Section 3.3, for any given n and p it is also possible to assume that π and C might depend on the specific decision rule used by the individual to determine his optimal alternative after all the data collected $X = (X_1, X_2, \ldots, X_n)$ is already available to him. Corollary 2.3.1 (3) proves that under the assumption of homogeneous skills and for any given odd number $n = 2k + 1$, the most efficient decision rule is a simple majority rule d^0, i.e. for all n and p, $\pi(n, d^0; p) \geqslant \pi(n, d; p)$ where d is any monotonic and neutral decision rule. Combining this result with the assumption that the cost function C is independent of d and linear in n, we can reduce problem (8.2.1) to a more explicit form. More specifically, if $C = \frac{1}{2}c(n + e)$ where c and e are non-negative constants which might be taken as non-decreasing functions of p, then problem (8.2.1) might be written as

$$(8.2.2) \quad \max_k \left[B \sum_{i=k+1}^{2k+1} \binom{2k+1}{i} p^i (1 - p)^{2k+1-i} - ck \right]$$

Since for $p > \frac{1}{2}$, $d\pi/dk > 0$ and $d^2\pi/dk^2 < 0$, problem (8.2.2) has a unique solution k^* which is the intersection point between the marginal revenue of consulting $Bd\pi/dk$ and the constant marginal cost c. Unsurprisingly, it is also evident that $dk^*/dB \geqslant 0$ and $dk^*/dc \leqslant 0$ as is already realized in Chapter 3. To illustrate, consider the same numerical example as used in Section 3.2.

Assuming that $B = 1$, $p = 0.8$ and $c = 0.03$, the following table presents the numerical values of the probability π and the expected net benefit V corresponding to one-, three- and five-member groups using the simple majority rule.

k	n	$\pi(n, d^0; 0.8)$	$V(n, d^0; 0.8) = B\pi - C$
0	1	0.800	0.800
1	3	0.896	0.806
2	5	0.946	0.796

Although the use of five consultants instead of three increases the probability of a correct decision from 0.896 to 0.946, the total net benefit V decreases from 0.806 to 0.796 because of the increasing cost. Since the cost is linear in k and the benefit is concave in k, any additional increase in k would further reduce the total net benefit V so that the optimal (non-sequential) demand for consulting services is, in this case, $n^* = 3$. As is well known, such a non-sequential procedure is not the most efficient one in the sense that the expected net benefit $V(n, d; p)$ might further be raised. Before demonstrating this point as a generality we shall first illustrate it by means of a couple of examples.

Consider a two-stage procedure of the following kind: Utilize the services of two consultants and follow their advice only on a unanimity basis. In case of conflicting recommendations, take three more consultants and use a simple majority rule to reach a final decision. In this case n is either 2 or 5, but on the average it is less than 3. Specifically

$$Em = 2[0.8^2 + 0.2^2] + 5[0.8(0.2) + 0.2(0.8)] = 2(0.68) + 5(0.32) = 2.98$$

The probability of a correct decision is

$$\frac{0.64}{0.68}0.68 + [0.8^3 + 3(0.8^2)0.2]0.32 = 0.64 + (0.896)0.32 = 0.927$$

the corresponding expected net benefit is

$$B\pi - cEm = 0.927 - (0.03)2.98 = 0.838$$

We see that by using a sequential technique we can both enlarge the probability of a correct decision and reduce the expected utilization of consulting services.

Using the same logic we can further increase the probability of a correct decision as well as lower the expected amount of consulting services by simply continuing the process instead of stopping at the second stage. Take at each step a pair of consultants and terminate the process only when one pair offers unanimous advice. In such a case, which might be termed the case of sequential simple majority rule, the probability of a correct decision is 0.941 and $Em = 2.94$, and the corresponding expected net benefit is further increased to 0.853.[1] As we shall see, under certain circumstances, this last procedure is also the optimal one.

8.2.2 The sequential version

In order to formulate the individual's problem of selecting an optimal stopping rule, we shall first transform the individual's dilemma into a hypotheses testing form. The individual's problem is to select one and only one of the following two symmetrical hypotheses

$$H_0 : \Pr\{X_i = 1\} = p \qquad (a \text{ is optimal})$$
$$H_1 : \Pr\{X_i = 1\} = 1 - p \quad (b \text{ is optimal})$$

The symmetry of the two alternatives implies that the individual is indifferent concerning the two error types. Suppose that the individual wishes to be protected so that the probability of error (of any kind) is at most $1 - \pi$, i.e.

(8.2.3) $\Pr\{\text{accept } H_0 | H_1\} \leqslant 1 - \pi$
$\Pr\{\text{accept } H_1 | H_0\} \leqslant 1 - \pi$

His problem is to choose a sequential procedure, or a stopping rule d, such that Em would be minimized subject to (8.2.3). This problem has a well-known solution in the literature of sequential analysis. We use this solution to solve the more general problem of finding a sequential process d such that for any given p it would solve

$$(8.2.4) \quad \max_d \left[B\pi - \frac{c}{2} Em \right]$$

where Em is the expected amount of consulting which can be taken as a function of π and d.

Consider the equation

$$(8.2.5) \quad \frac{B(2p-1)l(p)}{c} = l(\pi) + \frac{(2\pi - 1)}{2\pi(1 - \pi)}$$

and denote by π_0 the solution to (8.2.5) where B, p and c are constants and $l(y)$ is the logarithm of the odds of y, i.e.

$$l(y) = \ln \frac{y}{1 - y}$$

Note that since the LHS of (8.2.5) is positive and independent of π, while the RHS of (8.2.5) is equal to zero for $\pi = \frac{1}{2}$, but is a strictly increasing and convex function of π when $\frac{1}{2} < \pi < 1$, there always exists a unique solution π_0. As is established in Theorem 8.2.1 the value π_0 is a cornerstone of the solution to problem (8.2.4).

Theorem 8.2.1 The solution to (8.2.4) is given by the following stopping rule: Proceed with the consulting process if and only if

$$-\lambda < 2 \sum_{i=1}^{m} X_i - m < \lambda$$

for all $m = 1, \ldots, n$. Choose alternative a if

$$2 \sum_{i=1}^{n} X_i - n \geqslant \lambda$$

and choose alternative b if

$$2 \sum_{i=1}^{n} X_i - n \leqslant -\lambda, \quad \text{where } \lambda = \frac{l(\pi_0)}{l(p)}$$

This optimal procedure implies that

$$Em = \lambda \frac{\pi_0 - (1 - \pi_0)}{p - (1 - p)}$$

Proof: First note that the best test for H_0 against H_1 is the sequential probability ratio test (SPRT) as obtained by Wald (1947) and Lehman (1959), i.e. reject H_0 if $f_1(X)/f_0(X) > D$ and, since the problem is symmetric, accept H_0 if $f_0(X)/f_1(X) > D$ where D is a constant chosen in such a way that (8.2.3) holds. As long as $D^{-1} < f_1(X)/f_0(X) < D$ proceed with the consulting process.

$$\frac{f_1(X)}{f_0(X)} = \prod_{i=1}^{n} (1-p)^{x_i} p^{1-x_i} \bigg/ \prod_{i=1}^{n} p^{x_i}(1-p)^{1-x_i} = \left[\frac{(1-p)}{p}\right]^{2\Sigma x_i - n}$$

or

$$\ln\frac{f_0(X)}{f_1(X)} = \left(2\sum_{i=1}^{n} X_i - n\right) l(p)$$

So, for given π and p, the optimal sequential decision rule is SPRT: accept H_0 if

$$2\sum_{i=1}^{n} X_i - n \geqslant \lambda$$

and accept H_1 if

$$2\sum_{i=1}^{n} X_i - n \leqslant -\lambda$$

and continue the consulting process if and only if

$$-\lambda < 2\sum_{i=1}^{m} X_i - m < \lambda \quad \text{for all } m = 1,\ldots,n$$

The process must terminate at a finite stage, since, for every λ, the probability that n is finite is unitary (Stein, 1946). That is, the sequential decision process is almost always decisive. Given this procedure, we obtain

(8.2.6) $\quad E(2\Sigma X - m) = 2E(\Sigma X) - Em = \pi\lambda + (1-\pi)(-\lambda)$

But, by Wald's lemma, $E(\Sigma X) = pEm$ (Wald, 1947).
Substitute pEm for $E(\Sigma X)$ in (8.2.6) and solve for Em to find that

(8.2.7) $\quad Em = \lambda\dfrac{\pi - (1-\pi)}{p - (1-p)}$

By the martingale optimal stopping theorem (Lehmann, 1959), $1 = E(f_1/f_0)$. In our case

$$E\left(\frac{f_1}{f_0}\right) = E\left(\frac{1-p}{p}\right)^{2\Sigma X - n} = (1-\pi)\left(\frac{1-p}{p}\right)^{-\lambda} + \pi\left(\frac{1-p}{p}\right)^{\lambda} = 1$$

or

$$1 - \left(\frac{1-p}{p}\right)^{\lambda} = (1-\pi)\left[\left(\frac{1-p}{p}\right)^{-\lambda} - \left(\frac{1-p}{p}\right)^{\lambda}\right]$$

$$= (1-\pi)\left(\frac{1-p}{p}\right)^{-\lambda}\left[1 - \left(\frac{1-p}{p}\right)^{2\lambda}\right]$$

Multiply the last equation by

$$\left(\frac{1-p}{p}\right)^{\lambda} \Big/ \left[1 - \left(\frac{1-p}{p}\right)^{\lambda}\right]$$

to get

$$\left(\frac{1-p}{p}\right)^{\lambda} = (1-\pi)\left[1 + \left(\frac{1-p}{p}\right)^{\lambda}\right]$$

or

$$\left(\frac{1-p}{p}\right)^{\lambda} = \frac{1-\pi}{\pi}$$

Solve for λ to see that

(8.2.8) $\lambda = \dfrac{l(\pi)}{l(p)}$

Substitute (8.2.8) into (8.2.7) and then (8.2.7) into (8.2.4) to find that (8.2.4) is equivalent to

(8.2.9) $\max\limits_{\pi}\left[B\pi - c\,\dfrac{l(\pi)\,\pi - (1-\pi)}{l(p)\,p - (1-p)}\right]$

By taking the derivative of the expression in the brackets of (8.2.9) with respect to π and equating it to zero it can be easily verified that π_0 which maximizes (8.2.9) also solves (8.2.5).

We now present a few concluding remarks.

(a) Special cases of sequential procedures
If $p \geqslant \pi$, then $\lambda \leqslant 1$ and $Em \leqslant 1$ and the optimal procedure is to consult a single consultant only and take his advice. It can readily be verified that this is a degenerate case which is obtained by (8.2.5) if, for instance, the consulting fee c is very large relative to the net benefit B.

The sequential simple majority rule is obtained when $\lambda = 2$. The sequential procedure for which λ is an integer larger than 2 can be called a symmetric sequential qualified majority rule. Such a rule is a generalization of the non-sequential qualified majority rule that is investigated in Chapter 4.

Reconsider the simple majority rule of the example closing the discussion on the non-sequential version. We can now verify that by (8.2.8), if $p = 0.8$, then $\pi = 0.941$ and $Em = 2.94$. If $p = 0.75$, then $\pi = 0.9$ and $Em = 3.2$.

The exact solution for the case where $B = 1$, $c = 0.03$ and $p = 0.8$ is $\pi_0 = 0.955$ for which $\lambda = 2.2$ and $Em = 3.3$, but indivisibility implies that in such a case $\lambda = 2$.

(b) Comparative statics

By total differentiation of (8.2.5) with respect to π it can be verified that $\partial \pi_0 / \partial B > 0$, $\partial \pi_0 / \partial C < 0$ and $\partial \pi_0 / \partial p > 0$. Since $\lambda = l(\pi_0)/l(p)$ we also obtain that $\partial \lambda / \partial B > 0$ and $\partial \lambda / \partial c < 0$. That is, the critical value determining the optimal stopping rule is directly related to the net benefit B and it is inversely related to the constant marginal cost c. Since $Em = \lambda[\pi_0 - (1 - \pi_0)]/[p - (1 - p)]$ we also get that $\partial Em / \partial B > 0$ and $\partial Em / \partial c < 0$. That is, the optimal expected amount of consulting services is directly (inversely) related to net benefit B (constant marginal cost c). Recall that an analogous result holds with respect to the sensitivity of the optimal investment in human capital (see Chapter 7).

Finally, note that the signs of $\partial \lambda / \partial p$ and $\partial Em / \partial p$ are ambiguous. This is due to the conflicting effects that a change in the consultants' decisional skill has on the numerator and denominator in (8.2.8).

(c) Asymmetric sequential procedures

It is quite easy to relax, at this stage, the assumption of complete symmetry as well. This leads to the use of non-symmetric decision rules. In the non-symmetric case we may distinguish between two kinds of errors having $1 - \pi_1$ and $1 - \pi_2$ as upper limits for the probabilities of the two error types. In turn, the optimal asymmetric sequential process will be defined by λ_1 and λ_2 as critical boundaries.

(d) Heterogeneous skills

Homogeneity of skills is one of the strongest assumptions of the model presented in this section. It is worthwhile to investigate some of the consequences of the relaxation of this assumption. If the consulting cost is independent of the consultants' skill levels, the values of p_i, then the individual's best policy is to start first with the most qualified advisor and to continue along a descending order of skills. The assumption that the cost is the same for advisors with different qualifications is not so strong in cases where the consulting cost mainly comprises indirect cost, and only in small portion the direct consulting fee. In the case of heterogeneous consultants the criterion for the best stopping rule hinges on

$$2 \sum_{i=1}^{m} l(p_i) X_i - m$$

instead of

$$2 \sum_{i=1}^{m} X_i - m$$

In other words, instead of using sequential simple (or qualified) majority rules, the individual will use sequential *weighted* simple (or qualified) majority rules where the weights are increasing functions of skill. The rationale for taking

$$l(p_i) = \ln \frac{p_i}{(1 - p_i)}$$

as the most appropriate weights is given in Chapter 2 for the non-sequential case.

(e) Mean-variance (risk-aversion) considerations

Denote by π^* and n^* the maximal probability and the optimal amount of consulting in the non-sequential case respectively. It has to be emphasized that even if $\pi_0 > \pi^*$ and $Em < n^*$, the additional gain in expected benefit in the sequential case might be at the expense of additional risk. Adopting the mean–variance approach within which risk is measured by the variance, we can compare the two different optimal decision-making techniques by the following criteria:

	Mean	Variance
Non-sequential	$B\pi^* - \dfrac{c}{2} n^*$	$B^2 \pi^* (1 - \pi^*)$
Sequential	$B\pi_0 - \dfrac{c}{2} Em$	$B^2 \pi_0 (1 - \pi_0) + \left(\dfrac{c}{2}\right)^2 \sigma_m^2$

If the consulting fee c is high enough (relative to B) and if the individual is a high risk-averter (he assigns a higher weight to the variance relative to that of the mean) he might still give up the additional gain in expected net benefit and be content with a non-sequential procedure. We may therefore conclude that even when sequential decision processes are feasible, dispensing of the non-sequential rules might be premature given that individual attitudes toward risk are reflected by their utilities.

CHAPTER 9

Many alternatives and mixed rules

9.1   Introduction

This monograph focuses on a dichotomous choice situation where individuals or groups select a single element from a set consisting of only two alternatives. The assumption regarding the dichotomous nature of the choice problem seems to be a serious restriction, especially from the viewpoint of economists who usually deal with choice problems with a continuum of alternatives or, in the discrete case, with the multiple alternative situation. In particular, many interesting facets of social choice theory appear only when the set of alternatives consists of three or more alternatives.

The subsequent section discusses some possible justifications for the intensive effort made herein to study the special case of dichotomous choice.

The assumption of dichotomous choice considerably simplifies our analysis. It is also hard to deny that pairwise choice situations occur quite frequently in real decisional contexts. Besides the convenience of simplicity associated with the assumption and the fact that it is far from being a totally contrived simplification, Section 9.2 provides some arguments that attempt to clarify why the dichotomous choice situation deserves examination in its own right. Section 9.3 relaxes the pairwise choice assumption and reports one possible generalization of the main optimality result obtained under the basic model of Chapter 2.

A decisive decision rule is defined in Chapter 2 as a function from the domain of all decision profiles $\{1, -1\}^n$ into the range $\{1, -1\}$ where 1 and -1 represent the two available alternatives the group confronts. In the preceding chapter the definition of a decisive decision rule is generalized. Specifically, a sequential decision process is defined. Nevertheless, the final outcome of such a process is again one of the two available alternatives. The analysis undertaken up to this stage is thus confined to pure individual strategies and pure decision rules. That is, individual as well as collective choice directly terminates with the selection of one or the other alternative. It is well known that in game theory the optimal strategy for the individual player might turn out to be a mixed strategy rather than a pure strategy. Likewise, a collective decision rule yielding non-deterministic outcomes, namely collective lotteries, might be more appropriate than a pure social decision rule (see, for example, Zeckhauser (1969), Barbera and Valenciano (1983), Fishburn (1973), Fishburn and Gehrlein (1977a)). A lottery outcome on the two alternatives can be thought of as a process that selects alternative a with probability α and alternative b with probability $(1 - \alpha)$. Two natural questions therefore arise. First, given pure individual decision profiles, what is the justification for concentrating on pure decision rules rather than dealing with the more general class of non-deterministic decision rules that generate lotteries on the alternatives? Second, given individual mixed strategies on the alternatives, what is the optimal procedure to aggregate the individual strategies? Section 9.4 addresses the first issue. It is shown, under quite general conditions, that extending the basic model by allowing mixed decision rules cannot increase the group probability of making a correct choice. The second issue is finally discussed in Section 9.5. We survey a few recent studies all dealing with the problem of aggregating or combining individual mixed strategies (expert probabilistic evaluations). As will become evident, the last word on this type of generalization is far from being said.

9.2   Why binary choice?

The basic model and its various extensions assume that each individual and, in turn, the group face a set of alternatives containing two elements. This pairwise choice assumption considerably simplifies the analysis of many of the issues the current study deals with. At the same time the dichotomous choice assumption is sufficient in order to point to the problematics of group decision making as viewed under the decision theory approach. Furthermore, the results obtained under this assumption provide significant insight regarding the possible resolution of the different issues associated with the optimization problem of the group. The next section demonstrates how the solution of the optimization problem the group faces, given the assumptions of the basic model described in Chapter 2, serves as an essential means for extending the model to a possible multiple-alternative situation. It is our view that the two-alternatives theory, besides constituting an opening chord in the decision theoretic variation on the main theme of 'desirable collective decision making', serves also as a leading or indicative tone for the more general multiple-alternative case. Presented below are two additional arguments purported to justify our initial focus on binary choice situations. The first argument is based on empirical considerations. The second one is established on theoretical grounds.

In a practical sense the case of two alternatives is of paramount importance since individuals and groups often concentrate their attention on two competing alternatives and since numerous choice procedures are used to resolve pairwise choice competitions. Furthermore, dichotomous choice situations are of paramount significance since it is very often the case that the more substantive or critical choice situations are of a binary nature. The following statement is supported by empirical evidence. When a critical decision has to be made the situation can usually be characterized as a dichotomous choice situation. Put differently, if an individual or a group face a choice problem that involves substantive, existential, far reaching or specially serious consequences or a considerable amount of risk, it is most likely that the choice problem is dichotomous. The converse statement is not claimed, that is, a binary choice problem is not necessarily a critical one. Numerous examples come to mind. For instance, an individual decides on whether to get married or not, marry a particular candidate or not, abide to a certain code of ethics or not, or in Hamlet's words: 'to be or not to be' given that physical or spiritual existence is threatened. On the group level, consider political bodies facing decision regarding a declaration of war, the development and usage of nuclear weapons or the conclusion of a peace treaty.

As noted by Grofman *et al.* (1983), dealing with dichotomous cases is warranted since many important decision rules for the multi-alternative case can be decomposed into sequences of pairwise choices. Farquharson (1969) calls such procedures binary ones. To use his words,

> Suppose that a set [of alternatives] is divided into two subsets, each subset into two further subsets, and so on until single outcomes are reached.
>
> Such a sequence of divisions may be depicted as a tree, the 'outcome tree'. Each of its forks corresponds to an outcome.
>
> Since each division is into two subsets, we may call such procedures 'binary'. The class of binary procedures includes those of Parliament, with 'Aye' and 'No' lobbies, and the usual committee method of voting on amendments to a motion. It also includes some electoral procedures, such as that whereby each candidate is considered in turn for acceptance, and the Scot's practice of election by paired comparisons, in which one candidate is excluded at each division.

When the choice problem involves many alternatives and individual choices satisfy the Luce 'choice axiom' (Luce, 1959), binary procedures such as the Standard Amendment procedure dominate other majoritarian procedures such as plurality voting, approval voting or successive and sequential runoff procedures. Thus, for example, in the case of three alternatives $\{a_1, a_2, a_3\}$, if

$$p(a_i|\{a_i, a_j\}) = \frac{p_i}{p_i + p_j} \quad \text{for all } i \neq j \text{ and } j = 1, 2, 3$$

where $p_i = p(a_i|\{a_1, a_2, a_3\})$, then the decision set should be partitioned into a series of distinct binary choices followed by a process of sequential elimination in order to get the best choice. So under Luce's axiom the attainment of optimal choice in a multiple-alternative problem is guaranteed when the problem is decomposed into basic binary problems. At any stage the results of the two alternatives theory can be applied interpreting $p(a_i|\{a_i, a_j\})$ as the individual skill parameter at that stage where alternatives a_i, a_j are confronted.

9.3   The multiple-alternative case

Suppose that the set of alternatives consists of m alternatives. Only one alternative is the best one with respect to the common interest of the n members of the group. That alternative is referred to as the correct choice. The other alternatives are called incorrect. Here each individual reports a linear[1] ordering on the alternatives, thus revealing his judgement as to the alternative most likely to be correct, the next most likely one, and so forth. An n-tuple of linear orders representing the group members' judgements is the decision profile analogue of the dichotomous context. We are concerned with collective decision making which is based on the individual judgements. Hence, a decision rule in the multiple-alternative case is a function from the set of all possible preference profiles to the set of non-empty subsets of alternatives. Let us represent individual i's competence $(i = 1,\ldots,n)$ by the vector $(p_{i1},\ldots,p_{im})$

$$\sum_{j=1}^{m} p_{ij} = 1$$

where the probability of the alternative that individual i ranks in the jth position to be the correct alternative is equal to $p_{ij}, j = 1,\ldots,m$. Confining our attention to cost-free neutral decision rules and assuming independence of individual judgements as well as invariance of net benefit of correct choice to the labeling of correct and incorrect alternatives,[2] we obtain a generalization of the basic dichotomous model of Chapter 2 to the multiple-alternative case. Within this extended basic model an optimal decision rule maximizes the expected common utility of the decision makers, or equivalently, the collective probability of making the correct choice. In other words, the optimal rule is a solution to a problem analogous to problem (2.2.1). Recently, Young (1983) addressed this more general problem. Following closely the proof of Theorem 2.3.1, Young finds that the maximum likelihood decision rule is a scoring rule defined by the scores

$$s_{ij} = \ln \frac{p_{ij}}{(1 - p_{ij})} \quad \text{for } i = 1,\ldots,n, j = 1,\ldots,m$$

The real number s_{ij} is the weight assigned to the alternative being in the jth position according to individual i's ranking. Given the n individual rankings of the m alternatives, the scoring rule selects the alternatives obtaining the largest total weight. For $m = 2$ the optimal scoring rule is the optimal weighted majority rule specified by Theorem 2.3.1. The analysis of the basic dichotomous choice situation is certainly indicative to that of the particular generalization discussed in this section. The more general result indeed illustrates the significance of dichotomous situations analysis, as such analysis may constitute a stepping-stone for the investigation of the more general multi-alternative contexts.

9.4   Lottery decision rules

The decision rules dealt with in the preceding chapters are decisive or pure decision rules. The set of pure decision rules for a group of n individuals confronting alternatives a and b is

$$F = \{f : f : \{1, -1\}^n \to \{1, -1\}\}$$

where 1 and -1 designate the selection of alternative a and alternative b respectively. The more general sequential rules discussed in Chapter 8 are also pure as eventually the decision process terminates in the decisive selection of one of the alternatives. A lottery decision rule is a natural generalization of a decisive decision rule. Specifically, the set of lottery decision rules is

$$L = \{l : l : \{1, -1\}^n \to [0, 1]\}$$

where $[0, 1]$ is the closed interval of real numbers between zero and one. For any decision profile $x = (x_1, \ldots, x_n)$ in $\{1, -1\}^n$, the function l assigns a lottery outcome on the two alternatives, namely alternative a is selected in probability $l(x)$ and alternative b is selected in probability $(1 - l(x))$. Obviously, F is a subset of L since F can be viewed as $F = \{l : \{1, -1\}^n \to \{1, 0\}\}$. Let us denote by $\pi(l, p)$ the collective probability of obtaining the correct outcome. The basic problem (2.2.1) can be rephrased as

$$(9.4.1) \quad \max_{l \in L^*} \pi(l, p)$$

where $L^* = \{l \in L : l \text{ is neutral}\}$.

As in the basic model, neutrality is required because of the symmetry of the alternatives. A lottery decision rule is *neutral* if for any decision profile x, $l(-x) = 1 - l(x)$.

The following theorem justifies our dealing with pure decision rules. It obviates the need to extend the set of pure decision rules to that of lottery decision rules by establishing that there always exists a pure decision rule belonging to the solution set of problem (9.4.1). That is, if $\hat{l}$ satisfies $\pi(\hat{l}, p) \geq \pi(l, p)$ for all l in L^*, then there exists a pure decision rule f in F such that $\pi(f, p) = \pi(\hat{l}, p)$. If the vector of competences p is such that there is no profile y in Ω where the probabilities to obtain y and $-y$ are equal, i.e. $g(y) = g(-y)$, then the above result can be strengthened; a solution to problem (9.4.1) must be a pure decision rule. The proof of the stronger version is presented below. The proof of the more general version which needs only a slight modification is omitted.

Theorem 9.4.1 If $\hat{l}$ satisfies $\pi(\hat{l}, p) \geqslant \pi(l, p) \forall l \in L^*$, then $\hat{l} \in F$ whenever p is such that $g(y) \neq g(-y) \forall y \in \Omega$.

Proof: Suppose, to the contrary, that $\hat{l} \notin F$. Then there is at least one profile x_0 for which both $g(x_0) > g(-x_0)$ and $\frac{1}{2} \leqslant \hat{l}(x_0) < 1$. Let us define a new decision rule l_0 in the following way.

$$l_0(x) = \begin{cases} \hat{l}(x) & \text{if } x \neq x_0 \text{ and } x \neq -x_0 \\ 1 & \text{if } x = x_0 \\ 0 & \text{if } x = -x_0 \end{cases}$$

It is clear that l_0 is also a member of L^*. By definition,

$$\pi(\hat{l}, p) = \sum_{x \in \Omega} g(x)\hat{l}(x)$$

and

$$\pi(l_0, p) = \sum_{\substack{x \neq x_0 \\ x \neq -x_0}} g(x)\hat{l}(x) + g(x_0)$$

So that

$$\pi(l_0, p) - \pi(\hat{l}, p) = g(x_0) - [g(x_0)\hat{l}(x_0) + g(-x_0)(1 - \hat{l}(x_0))] > 0$$

a contradiction to the optimality of $\hat{l}$.

9.5   Aggregation of individual probability assessments

Suppose that a group of individuals, each being a Bayesian, is required to make a joint decision. Members of the group may share the same preferences regarding a given set of alternatives, yet disagree on the prior distribution of the relevant states of nature. What is the desirable mode of aggregating the group members' priors? This problem of combining probability judgements has attracted a great deal of attention. Scholars recently addressing this problem (Morris, 1974, 1977, 1983; Madansky, 1978; Bordley, 1982; Barrett and Pattanaik, 1983) take different axiomatic approaches and provide different solutions to the problem. For instance, Barrett and Pattanaik prove a sort of impossibility theorem: only trivial aggregation procedures satisfy a certain set of plausible conditions. Other scholars suggest the arithmetic or geometric mean of either the individual probabilities or their odds as the appropriate method of aggregation.

The probability aggregation problem differs from the problem of individual decisions aggregation based on the individual proficiencies in several fundamental respects. The problem of aggregating expert probability assessments deals with the multiple-alternative situation. It is concerned with the selection of collective probability assessments given individuals that are characterized by their personal evaluation of alternatives (their priors), rather than by their strict attitudes regarding the correct alternative. Finally, no information is assumed with respect to the skills of the experts. Nevertheless, under a binary choice context the optimal aggregation of priors is related to the optimal decision rule derived in Chapter 2 (Bordley, 1982).

CHAPTER 10

Applications

10.1   Introduction

The basic uncertain dichotomous choice model, as well as its various extensions, have numerous potential applications in a variety of fields. We have already seen a few examples such as the demand for consulting services in a non-sequential set up (Chapter 3) as well as in a sequential context (Chapter 8), or the justification for particular qualified majority rules in political bodies of different size, skill and bias toward the status quo (Chapter 4). The current chapter presents three more applications of the model taken from different worlds of contents: medicine, law and industrial organization. The medical example in Section 10.2 is based on real data collected in a hospital. This application is concerned with the efficiency of a cardiac diagnostic system used by a panel of three experts. It clearly points to some of the difficulties faced while attempting to apply the stylized basic model. Section 10.3 deals with the legal relationships between stockholders and corporate boards. Here the application of our analysis sheds new light on the debate about cumulative voting versus the common law. Section 10.4 focuses on aspects of industrial organization of the services sector. More specifically, an attempt is made to answer the question of why partnership, as a form of economic organization, is more popular in some industries within the services sector while it occurs less frequently in others. Without refuting other attempts prevailing in the economic literature, the analysis of an extended version of our basic model provides additional insight into this question. We argue that partnerships are justly more frequent in the consulting services, relative to other services industries, and that this form of organization is especially needed under circumstances rendering sequential decision processes highly expensive.

10.2   A medical application

The major difficulty in applying the model involves the objective estimation of the experts' skills. Let us turn now to a detailed medical application whereby such estimation of experts' abilities has been attempted.

Grading the accuracy and excellence of medical care may be an almost impossible task. Overall estimation may be somewhat easier than the evaluation of an individual case history. The performance of a surgeon is judged by the percentage of mortality and complications. Thus the death of a patient does not necessarily mean that the surgery was bad. A mortality rate of 10% in a coronary care unit (provided proper criteria are used for the diagnosis of acute myocardial infarction) denotes excellent medical care.

Objective grading may be somewhat more feasible when applied to the judgement of a physician's diagnostic acumen. How many times will he or she make a correct diagnosis on the basis of the patient's medical history, physical examination, electrocardiogram and routine X-ray before advanced and sophisticated laboratory studies yield definitive results?

In the light of this observation we examined the diagnostic ability of a group of three cardiologists from the Department of Cardiology, Meir Hospital, Kfar-Saba, Israel. Our findings are based on a sample of 362 consecutive cases during the period 1975–9. The patients in the sample suffered from non-coronary forms of heart disease, including endocardial, myocardial, peri-cardial and valvular lesions both congenital and acquired. Each patient was examined only by one cardiologist prior to cardiac catheterization, a procedure enabling accurate diagnosis of congenital and valvular lesions of the heart. By comparing the pre- and post-catheterization diagnoses, a diagnostic score could be established.

This scoring procedure, however, raised a couple of problems:

(1) How accurate had the doctor to be to achieve a full score? What if he diagnosed two out of three lesions, or produced a correct diagnosis but misjudged the severity?
(2) There may be lesions that do not render themselves to clinical diagnosis, and whose true nature can be revealed only by cardiac catheterization.

We therefore decided to give the cardiologist the full score of 1 when the catheterization confirmed the main clinical diagnosis and thus warranted a continuation of the pre-catheterization management plan. A mistake of severity large enough to effect a change in the management of the disease was regarded as a diagnostic error despite the fact that the specific lesion was recognized before catheterization. An incorrect diagnosis earned a score of 0.

The second problem was disregarded: namely, an incorrect diagnosis was scored as such regardless of the inherent difficulties. When more than 33 percent but less than 100 percent of the lesions were diagnosed, diagnosis was considered partially correct. A partially correct decision was given a score of 0.5.

Of the 362 diagnoses, 249 were correct, 63 were partially correct and 50 were incorrect. The simple average score thus amounted to

$$\frac{(249 \times 1) + (63 \times 0.5) + (50 \times 0)}{362} = \frac{280.5}{362} = 0.77$$

The data did not enable us to estimate the abilities of the individual cardiologists since, although each patient was examined by one expert, no complete record of identities of diagnosticians was available. We have, therefore, followed the department head's assessment and assumed equality of skills among the three cardiologists. Under this assumption the cardial diagnostic system in the Meir Hospital is equivalent to the single-chief-expert rule whereby the decision is left in the hands of one (the most qualified) decision maker. This rule is a reasonable weighted majority rule that is defined by the vector of weights $(w_1, w_2, w_3) = (1, 0, 0)$. The resultant probability of obtaining a correct diagnosis is equal to $\pi_1 = p_1 = 0.77$. In a symmetric dichotomous diagnosis situation, simple majority rule is the only alternative to the expert rule. Under the former system two distinct diagnoses are put to a vote and the panel of three cardiologists selects the one that receives more votes. This alternative reasonable weighted majority rule can be defined by the vector $(w_1, w_2, w_3) = (1, 1, 1)$.

The probability of a correct diagnosis under the simple majority diagnostic system is

$$\pi_2 = p_1 p_2 p_3 + (1 - p_1) p_2 p_3 + p_1 (1 - p_2) p_3 + p_1 p_2 (1 - p_3)$$

and in our case

$$\pi_2 = (0.77)^3 + 3(0.23)(0.77)^2 = 0.87$$

That is, the diagnostic performance of the three cardiologists can be substantially improved by adopting the simple majority system. More precisely, the current probability of making a correct diagnosis can be increased by 0.10 once the alternative diagnostic system (simple majority rule) is adopted. Finally, in the case of equally skilled experts $p_1 = p_2 = p_3 = p$, the advantage of majority rule over the expert rule is equal to

$$\pi_2 - \pi_1 = p^3 + 3p^2(1 - p) - p$$
$$= -2p^3 + 3p^2 - p$$

For $p > 0.5$ this function is concave and it reaches its maximum value at $p = 0.788$. That is, the largest possible advantage for majority rule over the expert rule is obtained under moderate common expertise $p_1 = p_2 = p_3 =$

0.788. In this case $\pi_2 - \pi_1 = 0.107$. We thus conclude that if the probability of a correct diagnosis is the only concern, then one of the strongest possible cases has been made for the adoption of the simple majority diagnostic system by our panel of three cardiologists. This conclusion still holds if 10 percent of B (the additional benefit) is larger than $c(3) - c(1)$ (the additional cost) where $c(n)$ is the cost involved in using n independent cardiologists with an expertise level of 0.77 in the diagnostic process.

10.3 A legal application: cumulative voting for directors versus the common law

10.3.1 Introduction

Under the common law, elections to corporate boards are held in the following manner: Names of the candidates are proposed in the stockholders' general meeting. A separate vote is counted for each candidate. Directors are elected to office if they carry the majority of the voting shares represented at the meeting. This method enables the majority to vote down all minority nominations; all open slots are filled by majority candidates.

This system of elections still prevails in many countries, including England and most Commonwealth jurisdictions. However, it has fallen from grace in several American states. By the last quarter of the nineteenth century, many American statesmen were greatly influenced by the recent political philosophy of John Stuart Mill, especially as presented in his book *Considerations on Representative Government* (1861) in which Mill praises the notion of proportional representation and denounces majoritarian absolutism as undemocratic. Though Mill was primarily concerned with the political arena, it seemed natural to apply his philosophy to the sphere of corporate governance. It was believed that the best method of ensuring proportional representation on corporate boards was the use of the elections mechanism known as 'cumulative voting'. Under this method, each stockholder is entitled to a number of votes equal to the number of his shares, multiplied by the number of directors to be elected. He may cast all his votes for a single director, or may distribute them among several candidates, as he sees fit. The candidates receiving the highest number of votes are elected to the board.

As cumulative voting was believed essential to a viable corporate de-mocracy, some legislators did not consider it sufficiently safe to entrust it to the goodwill and cooperation of potential incorporators. Rather, it was safely entrenched into state constitutions, with an implied prohibition against contracting away this 'basic right'. Many years later, the debate continued: does cumulative voting in fact ensure the achievement of important corporate-governance goals? If this is true, are they really so basic as to warrant compulsory state regulation? Or, do these goals more rightfully belong to the regular 'garden variety' of proprietory interests which, in a free enterprise system, should be allocated among the stockholders by freely negotiated contracts?

In this section, we propose to examine these issues by employing the basic model. Our main purpose is to compare the two rules on efficiency grounds in a well defined though quite stylized model. We characterize both cumulative voting and the common law as weighted majority rules. The basic difference between the two is that the common law can be a priori considered a weighted majority rule with a less diverse system of weights. In order to pursue the comparison between the two rules, we present a set of assumptions which, first, identify the particular weighted majority rules resulting from the usage of cumulative voting and the common law; secondly, describe the model which we propose as a stylized uncertain dichotomous choice model; and, finally, suggest the performance criterion for evaluating the two competing rules. The actual comparison between the two rules is then carried out. Our main result is that neither cumulative voting nor the common law is necessarily the 'better' rule. Either one can prove to be superior to the other, given different sets of conditions and circumstances. We attempt to define what these conditions and circumstances are.

We thus propose to substitute the current rhetoric propounded by both cumulative voting enthusiasts[1] and opponents for a more balanced, rigorous test, though admittedly a restricted one, for the relative merits of this method of electing corporate directors.

10.3.2 *The framework*

(a) **Weighted majority rules identification**

We have already mentioned that, regardless of the elections method, corporate decisions are reached in board meetings by employing a simple majority rule. This rule emanates from the law itself.[2] In practical effect, however, this simple majority rule can transform itself into a weighted majority rule, given the particular method for electing the directors and given the particular presumptions regarding the interdependence among the directors' decisions. It seems very reasonable to assume that, in general, cumulative voting and the common law will not result in identical weighted majority rules. This indeed is the case under the following two assumptions which enable us to identify the specific weighted majority rules associated with cumulative voting and the common law. These assumptions do not purport to reflect precisely the real-life decision-making processes in all actual boards. But it seems that they both qualify, as reasonable approximations, and prove to be quite useful in characterizing the basic differences between the two election systems.

Assumption 1 Under the common law, the largest faction of stockholders elects all members of the board.

This assumption is especially plausible in large, publicly held corporations. Assume, for example, that one group owns 5 percent of the stock, but all other proprietors are tiny and are scattered geographically. It is not likely that any of the small proprietors would be able to amass a sufficient number of votes to successfully oppose candidates proposed by the largest faction. If that largest faction is initially installed in incumbency, resulting in control of the proxy mechanism, the chances of smaller factions to run successful election campaigns are virtually reduced to nil.

A weaker form of our assumption is the assertion that under the common law one group of people, whether it constitutes the largest faction of stockholders or not, is able to elect all the members of the board. This weaker assumption is quite sufficient for the construction of our application, and seems to be rather well entrenched in empirical studies.[3]

The following second assumption applies under both the common law and cumulative voting.

Assumption 2 Directorial factions correspond with the existing factions in the constituency and each directorial faction presents a united front in all board decision-making processes.

The psychological motivation which lurks behind this assumption is that on many occasions directors are not oblivious to the concerns of the special interest groups which ascended them to incumbency. On occasion, especially in the case of smaller companies, controlling stockholders and corporate office holders are in fact the same persons. In the larger enterprises, in which directors are hired career technocrats with no substantial stock ownership of their own, their destinies are often determined by direct reference to their performance, as judged by the one-sided gauge of a special interest group. A practical implication of this phenomenon is that we may expect Assumption 2 to be satisfied: Directorial factions will correspond with the existing factions in the constituency, and a united front in important board struggles will be presented by each directorial faction.

What is the impact of the formation of directorial factions upon the process of decision making within the board? Two significant features are immediately apparent. Firstly, the number of decision makers is reduced from the number of directors to the number of directorial factions. The plurality of human beings within each faction may be ignored, as they are all assumed to speak with a single voice. Secondly, since the law assigns one vote for each director regardless of his factional affiliation, factions can vote their positions several times, i.e. a number of times equal to the number of directors constituting the faction. In the contest among factions, a majority still prevails, but it is no longer a simple majority. Both cumulative voting and the common law are thus equivalent to weighted majority rules. In the contest among factions a certain proposal is passed by a weighted majority rule if the total weight of its supporters exceeds the total weight of the factions opposing it. Given Assumptions 1 and 2 the particular weighted majority rules corresponding to the common law and to cumulative voting can now be identified. Under the common law the largest faction of stockholders appoints the entire board and so the board may be regarded as consisting of a sole directorial faction. As other groups are not represented, and since the controlling directorial faction is assumed to abide by a single allegiance, the common law creates a weighted majority rule which can be termed 'the dictatorial rule' or 'the expert rule'. Under this rule the largest faction of directors is assigned a positive weight and weights of all other factions are zero. Cumulative voting, on the other hand, is a more flexible rule, as it does not always engender the same type of a rule, namely the dictatorial rule. True, sometimes it can result in assigning a positive weight to only one faction. This occurs whenever one directorial faction enjoys more than 50 percent support in the constituency. In this special case cumulative voting and the common law both result in dictatorial corporate regimes and are theoretically indistinguishable. But cumulative voting may assign positive weights to several directorial factions. In those cases board decisions are reached by employing a weighted majority rule different from the expert rule, where the weights are, roughly speaking, equal to the interests among the stockholders.

(b) Uncertain dichotomous choice

In the remainder of this section we confine our analysis to dichotomous choice situations. That is:

Assumption 3 The board faces two distinct alternatives at a time and a clear cut decision is made between the two.

Let us denote by $N = \{1,\dots,n\}$ the set of directorial factions choosing between the two alternatives a and b. Every directorial faction, or a representative of a faction, selects one of the two choices. The board voting profile is $(x_1,\dots,x_n)$ where $x_i = 1$ or $x_i = -1$ according to the actual choice of faction i. The decision rule f transforms individual decisions into that single alternative which is selected as the corporate course of actions. The decisive decision rules engendered by the common law and by cumulative voting are denoted respectively by f^{cl} and f^{cv}. In the light of Assumptions 1, 2 and 3, both f^{cv} and f^{cl} are decisive weighted majority rules. Recall that, by Assumption 1, f^{cl} is defined by a set of weights assigning zero to all but one of the factions in the constituency. f^{cv} can be characterized, of course, by any non-negative set of weights depending on the ownership pattern of the firm.

We now turn to the completion of the model by relating to the preferences and abilities of the directorial factions under conditions of uncertainty.

Assumption 4 The selection of one of the alternatives constitutes the common will of the stockholders. That alternative is referred to as the 'correct alternative'. The prior odds as to which of the two alternatives is the correct one are even.

This assumption requires that all stockholders in a given corporation have the same business goal in mind. This goal is the maximization of the common utility of all stockholders, which may be interpreted, *inter alia*, as the maximization of profit. While we realize that this assumption is not without its drawbacks, we believe it to be far more acceptable in the corporate context than in several other social-choice situations, in which individuals strain to attain different social goals. Where unanimity of purpose prevails, the problem of corporate boards is to adopt common utility-maximizing decisions under conditions of uncertainty. In our model we parameterize the decisional skill of faction i by the probability p_i of identifying the correct alternative.

Assumption 5 The values of p_i are statistically independent. Thus, the ability of directorial faction i is not affected by how other factions actually vote. The vector $(p_1, \ldots, p_n)$ represents the qualifications of the directors. The performance of the board to which we can now turn will in general depend on the vector of skills as well as on the vector of weights defining the actual weighted majority rule adopted by the board.

(c) Performance criterion

Assumption 6 Decisive decision rules are compared in terms of their respective probabilities for securing the selection of the correct alternative.

Various possible criteria can be utilized in order to compare alternative decision rules. The most common one is the expected utility criterion. Recall that if we assume that the two alternatives are symmetric (in addition to being a priori equiprobable, the loss incurred by an incorrect decision is the same regardless of whether alternative a or alternative b is mistakenly chosen), then the expected utility criterion is equivalent to the criterion suggested in Assumption 6, namely using the probability of selecting the correct alternative as a performance criterion.[4] Given the set of Assumptions 1–6 we are ready for the comparison between f^{cl} and f^{cv}.

10.3.3 *Is cumulative voting superior to the common law?*

(a) Is either rule optimal?

To recapitulate, both cumulative voting and the common law result in decisive weighted majority rules. The optimal amongst such rules is the one yielding the maximal probability π of identifying the correct alternative for the board's particular given set of qualifications. Theorem 2.3.1 identifies the optimal weighted majority rule. Namely, given assumptions 3, 4 and 5 the weighted majority rule which maximizes the probability π is defined by the set of weights $(\beta_1, \ldots, \beta_n)$ where

$$\beta_i = \ln \frac{p_i}{1 - p_i}$$

Note that $(\beta_1, \ldots, \beta_n)$ need not characterize either f^{cv} or f^{cl}; although neither rule is necessarily optimal, one system can of course be closer to optimality than the other. In the following few paragraphs we juxtapose cumulative voting and the common law in search of the better solution.

(b) Where the difference counts

The common law and cumulative voting may yield an identical probability of reaching correct decisions. For example, consider the case where the largest faction commands an absolute majority of all voting shares. In this case the largest directorial faction under cumulative voting, as well as the only faction under the common law, reigns supreme. Minorities have no (formal) impact on the decision-making process.

The two systems may yield, however, non-identical probabilities of success. This occurs whenever the largest faction commands less than half of all voting shares. Under cumulative voting (but not under the common law), minorities must be consulted to ensure a winning coalition on the board.

Let us turn therefore to the comparison between the two systems where the difference counts; that is, we confine our analysis to cases where it is possible that no faction is supported by an absolute majority of the stockholders, and thus different weighted majority rules are associated with cumulative voting and the common law. It is worthwhile mentioning that, in the realm of publicly held corporations, only rarely does a single proprietor control the absolute majority of the voting stock. Our analysis is, therefore, meaningful to the vast majority of public corporations.

(c) Ownership structure and directors' professional skills are known

If directors' qualifications as well as the directorial factions' weights are known, one can simply compute the probabilities of correct choice associated with cumulative voting and the common law, and then make an intelligent choice between the two systems. For instance, suppose there are three factions, 1, 2 and 3, that hold 40 percent, 35 percent and 25 percent of the stock respectively, and that weights are proportional to holdings. Cumulative voting thus yields a simple majority rule, since any two-faction coalition is winning. If the factions' values of p_i are 0.85, 0.70 and 0.55 respectively, then the corporation is better off by letting the largest faction decide for the board rather than applying the simple majority rule generated by cumulative voting. In the former case, the probability of a correct decision is equal to $p_1 = 0.85$, which is larger than 0.793 – the probability of obtaining the correct alternative under the latter case.[5] We thus obtain that the common law yields the better outcome. Suppose now that the board qualifications are given by 0.85, 0.80, 0.75. Here cumulative voting results in better performance, since the probability of correct decision under the majority rule is 0.898, which is larger than 0.85 – the success probability of correct decision under the expert rule. To sum up, if we only knew the particular weights associated with f^{cl} and f^{cv} and the qualifications of the directorial factions, we could point with certainty to the better rule. A similar conclusion holds under certain special cases where the ownership pattern of the corporation is unknown. Three such illustrations are given in the next section.

(d) Directors' skills are known – ownership pattern is unknown

Consider a situation where it is known that the largest faction is blessed with a dominant candidate who never makes mistakes, i.e. $p_1 = 1$. Obviously, in this case the rule which maximizes the probability of choosing correctly (the optimal rule) is a dictatorial rule of the clairvoyant – the expert rule. Cumulative voting might subject this person to an undesirable need to form coalitions with possibly erring individuals who may arm-twist the corporation into unfortunate board decisions. Even though clairvoyance is a rather extreme situation, it helps to clarify our point: Minorities ought to be ignored where the representatives of the largest faction are so talented as to render tampering with corporate affairs by less qualified individuals a liability rather than an asset. In other words, no matter what is the ownership pattern of the company, the optimal rule is the expert rule which is associated with the common law. More generally, by Corollary 2.3.1 (2), if

$$\beta_1 > \sum_{j=2}^{n} \beta_j$$

and given Assumptions 1–6, then f^{cl} is always at least as good as f^{cv}. The best that cumulative voting can generate (dependent on the ownership structure) is the same rule, and this proves the claim.

It is possible, on the other hand, that cumulative voting is preferable to the common law regardless of the ownership pattern. Assume, for instance, that all directors are identical in their personal qualifications. By Corollary 2.3.1 (3) and given Assumptions 1–6, we obtain that f^{cv} is always as good as f^{cl}. In this case f^{cl} turns out to be the least desirable rule. Therefore whatever weighted majority rule is generated for cumulative voting is at least as desirable as f^{cl} and hence the proof of the theorem is complete. In other words, relatively skilled equals ($p > \frac{1}{2}$) should not be subordinated to one of their midst, since a dictatorial collective decision rule produces, under these circumstances, inferior results relative to any further democratic weighted majority rule. In particular, any non-equal treatment of directors results in a non-optimal rule. No matter which particular weighted majority rule turns out to be associated with cumulative voting, it cannot be inferior to the expert rule. Therefore, cumulative voting is preferable to the common law in terms of its long-run expected performance.

Finally, let us reconsider the three-faction situation where $(p_1, p_2, p_3) = (0.85, 0.80, 0.75)$. Note that in this case, where $n = 3$ the set of decisive weighted majority rules consists of the three possible dictatorial rules and the common simple majority rule. In the preceding subsection we have demonstrated that, under a particular ownership structure, the common law is inferior to cumulative voting. In fact, the same conclusion holds true for any initial ownership pattern. The common law always yields the inferior rule, whereas cumulative voting may sometimes generate the optimal rule, so overall cumulative voting is superior to the common law.

These three special cases illustrate that information about professional skills might suffice to determine which is the preferable rule. The difficulty however is that under certain important circumstances complete information regarding skills (as well as the ownership pattern) is also lacking.

(e) Directors' skills are partially known

We do not really know the vector of personal skills and the vector of relative shares in one particularly important case – the initial or legislative stage. At that stage, we do not deal with identifiable companies, but rather with all existing companies and with all enterprises to be incorporated in the future. The persons who may be expected to run these enterprises are not determinable, and this holds true for their personal skills and stock ownership as well. Consequently, we cannot make a direct comparison between the two systems in this legislative stage. We can, however, make an indirect comparison if we are prepared to speculate either about the 'technology of skills' or, directly, about the nature of the distribution of professional skills.

Suppose that directors' skills are related to stock ownership by a function which is denoted by $p_i(\alpha)$ where $0 \leqslant (\alpha) \leqslant 1$ is the relative holdings of corporate stock. Let

$$p(\alpha) = \begin{cases} 0.90 & \alpha \geqslant 0.5 \\ 0.65 & \text{otherwise}^6 \end{cases}$$

and assume there are three stockholders whose particular weights and directorial skills are unknown. Despite such lack of information, it can certainly be asserted that cumulative voting is preferable to the common law. In fact, under the above 'technology of skills', cumulative voting always secures the optimal weighted majority rule. For, consider any possible ownership pattern $(\alpha_1, \alpha_2, \alpha_3)$, if $\alpha_1 > 0.50$, then $(p_1, p_2, p_3) = (0.90, 0.65, 0.65)$. In such a case cumulative voting and the common law generate the expert rule, which is indeed the optimal weighted majority rule. If $\alpha_1 < 0.50$, then $(p_1, p_2, p_3) = (0.65, 0.65, 0.65)$. In such a case cumulative voting, unlike the common law, generates the simple majority rule which is, again, the optimal weighted majority rule. To sum up, the 'technology of skills' can be so restricted as to guarantee the fulfilment of the necessary and sufficient conditions for the optimality of that weighted majority rule which is associated with cumulative voting, under any possible ownership structure.

In Section 10.3.3 (d) we have discussed two examples which stand for two diametrically opposed assumptions. In the first example there exists a sufficiently skilled directorial faction. In the second example directorial factions are equally skilled. Under the first example the common law is superior to cumulative voting and, in the second example, the reverse conclusion obtains. Having in mind these two examples, one is intuitively inclined to state the following heuristic proposition: Cumulative voting is superior to the common law where directors are sufficiently homogeneous, but the common law yields a better result where qualifications vary widely. The question is, of course, when are qualifications 'sufficiently homogeneous?' If the distribution of skills is symmetric with an average skill $\bar{p} > \frac{1}{2}$, then results analogous to Condorcet's Jury Theorem can be obtained.[7] This demonstrates that having only partial information on directors' skills might suffice to determine which of the two rules f^{cv} and f^{cl} should be preferred. Such partial information might be supported by subjective belief, possibly buttressed by prevailing egalitarian creeds; and of course, by statistical evidence regarding the distribution of skills in the population.

10.3.4 Conclusions

The following are the conclusions of this section:

(1) Under our stylized assumptions, cumulative voting differs from the common law only in the cases where no faction constitutes an absolute majority of stockholders. Where no absolute majority exists, the common

law is equivalent to a dictatorial rule. Cumulative voting, on the other hand, may translate itself to any possible weighted majority rule.

(2) The central issue in this section is which one of the two systems yields a larger probability that the board adopt common-utility maximizing measures. As it turns out, no system can claim an a priori advantage over the other. However, in the case where ownership of shares and qualifications are known, it can be precisely determined which is better. Furthermore, under certain special cases, the resolution of the dilemma is possible without resorting to information about ownership of shares. The resolution of the problem is also possible under certain circumstances of partial information concerning skills. Such partial information may be derived, for instance, from the estimation of the production function of skills or from the general nature of the distribution of skills in society. Roughly speaking, where qualifications vary widely, the expert rule engendered by the common law is the best available system. Where directors are sufficiently homogeneous in their professional skills, a strong case emerges for supporting the more egalitarian system of cumulative voting.

(3) Since without any information concerning either skills or the ownership distribution, the better system cannot be identified, it seems futile to coerce corporations to employ either cumulative voting or the common law. Legislators should thus abandon either extreme statutory mandate, and let firms opt for their own method of corporate governance. Within the firm a much more informed decision can be reached, since both skills and the ownership pattern can either be ascertained or at least intelligently speculated on. If a given firm should opt improvidently for the less efficient method, its error may be self-correcting through the market mechanism, since its lower profitability would render it, in the long run, less attractive to the investing public.

10.4　On the economic organization of the services sector

Economists noted long ago that the economic organization of the services sector follows a certain pattern. In some industries one can hardly find partnerships while in others a partnership is the most popular form of organization. For instance, partnerships are more frequent in accountancy than in hair styling. Alchian and Demsetz (1972, p. 790) offer an explanation:

Team production in artistic or professional intellectual skills will more likely be by partnerships than other types of team production. This amounts to market-organized team activity and to a nonemployer status. Self-monitoring partnerships, therefore, will be used rather than employer–employee contracts, and these organizations will be small to prevent an excessive dilution of efforts through shirking.

Without denying the importance of monitoring costs and the effects these have on economic organization, it is not a sufficient explanation in our case. It does not amount to the frequency distribution of partnerships across several branches of the services sector. Moreover, as is explicitly indicated by Leibowitz and Tollison (1980), the proposition of Alchian and Demsetz raises some questions and puzzles when tested against empirical data.

Other arguments such as managerial cost saving, cuts in insurance costs and possibilities for tax avoidance also seem to be unsatisfactory in providing general explanations, even if it is impossible to deny their significance in certain cases. We propose the following alternative thesis: any industry in which the consulting process might increase the user's expected benefit (via the probability of deciding correctly) has a relatively high proportion of partnerships. One can almost define this on a purely semantic basis. Whenever the consumption of a service is described by using the verb 'to consult' there is a high frequency of partnerships. We consult a lawyer and we consult a doctor, but we get a haircut and we go to the movies. It is quite evident that partnerships occur very frequently in the legal and medical professions, but not in the entertainment or hairdressing fields. In fact, most of the lawyers in the USA practice in partnerships, see Leibowitz and Tollison (1980, p. 381). Moreover, even within industries similar distinctions can be made. For instance, in dentistry and psychiatry there is a smaller proportion of partnerships than in surgery or orthopedics. It is in fields where one usually says: 'It's better to get another opinion' that partnerships are most likely to emerge. The reason for such a correlation between the organizational structure and the consulting element involved is twofold: first, a partnership is capable of providing a better advice than that of its most qualified member, and second, partnerships may save the clients consulting costs. This is a straightforward implication of the model presented in Chapters 2 and 3.

Denote by $\hat{\pi}(p, m)$ the probability of a correct decision being provided by a partnership of m members with a common skill level p and denote by $\hat{C}(p, m)$ the consulting fee charged by such a partnership. Similarly, let $\pi^*(p, m)$ and $C^*(p, m)$ denote the probability of correct choice and the decision making costs respectively, given m individuals with skill equal to p, however, no partnership arrangement is assumed. Then, even if $\pi^*(p, m) > \hat{\pi}(p, m)$ but $B\hat{\pi}(p, m) - \hat{C}(p, m) > B\pi^*(p, m^*) - C^*(p, m^*)$, the existence of such a partnership is fully justified and its survival is due to the additional welfare it provides. There is no necessary relationship between $\pi^*(p, m)$ and $\hat{\pi}(p, m)$, the two could be equal in the case that independence among members within the partnership is maintained and any decision is taken by simple majority rule, but $\hat{\pi}(p, m)$ could also be smaller or larger than $\pi(p, m)$. The important point is that $\hat{\pi}(p, m + 1) > \hat{\pi}(p, m)$. On the cost side it is most likely that $\hat{C}(p, m) < C^*(p, m)$. It is well known that the clustering phenomenon that is observed in many businesses, such as in shoes or electric appliances industries is explained by the saving of search costs on the part of the consumers. Analogously, a partnership of doctors or lawyers can be viewed as a cluster of consultants which exists to save consulting costs on the part of the clients. It has to be remembered that the consulting cost comprises not only the fee charged by the consultant but also the client's time needed to set up an appointment and to state his case, the shadow price of which possibly being, under emergency circumstances, extremely expensive. Another point that must be noted is the fact that partnerships of different sizes also enlarge the variety of probabilities for a successful decision from which the client can choose with respect to his possibilities for payment. So even if all consultants have the same skill p, partnerships of different sizes are entities which offer different probabilities in the range between p and 1. It is evident that the distribution by size of partnerships of lawyers ranges from two to sixty (see Leibowitz and Tollison (1980, p. 384)). The economic organization of the supply of consulting services into partnerships comes about in order to benefit the consumers by lowering consulting costs, as opposed to the situation where the clients have to gather consulting information via sequential procedures (see Chapter 8).

A partnership between members with non-homogeneous skills raises the question of free-riders, and so one can predict that, in general, the variance of skills within partnerships is smaller than between partnerships. In some cases a ranking system within the partnership is developed to differentiate among members. There are senior and junior members or some other keys for the allocation of profits according to skill.

There is no doubt that in many cases the skill level p is not a salient feature of the consultant and, therefore, the probability $\hat{\pi}(p,m)$ is only a latent characteristic of a partnership so that the decision-maker does not have accurate and full information about these probabilities, but even in these cases partial information may exist as well as signals that may indicate, at least in qualitative terms, the ability levels of the consultants or the consulting entities. Diplomas, years of experience, goodwill and reputation, to mention just a few, are some possible examples of such signals. Certainly, the signals assist the decision maker in assigning subjective probabilities to the several experts available to him in order to establish his optimal consulting process (see Chapter 5).

Finally, there is the assumption that opinions behave like independent drawings. Two comments are in order regarding this assumption. First, it should be noted that n consultants who work entirely independently might produce a *joint product* via the consulting process. The mere assumption of statistical independence implies a kind of externalities among consultants which raises π above p. Second, it is quite evident that in many partnerships this condition is unlikely to be satisfied, but here we must distinguish between two types of violation of this assumption. First, dependence might be generated by irrational and psychological effects such as charisma, leadership or persuasive talents. The result of such effects is a probability for correct decision which is smaller than the one which could be obtained under independence. Such a dependence is definitely inefficient and should be avoided among partners who share the same target function and do not have any conflict of interests. The effect of such interdependence is dealt with in Chapter 6. Second, there is an interaction process among experts which raises the experts' decisional skills. This type of interaction can be viewed as a learning process or as an investment in human capital that improves the ability to decide correctly. The effect of investment in human capital on the size of the decision group is studied in Chapter 7 and can be easily introduced into the model presented here by incorporating the costs of such an investment in human capital into the total consulting cost of the partnership.

Notes

Chapter 2: Uncertain dichotomous choice: the basic model

1 If only one of the two alternatives is irreversible this second requirement is unreasonable since type I and type II errors will often cause different losses. For instance, symmetry in the consequences of mistaken action and inaction might not be plausible in the criminal jury context; an unwarranted conviction might be considered worse than an objectionable acquittal.

2 Recall that $x_i = 1\,(-1)$ is interpreted as individual i selects the identified alternative a (alternative b), whereas $y_i = 1\,(-1)$ is interpreted as individual i selects the correct (incorrect) alternative. The fact that Ω denotes both a probability space and the set of all possible voting profiles should cause no confusions.

3
$$\text{sign}(z) = \begin{cases} 1 & z > 0 \\ -1 & z < 0 \\ 0 & z = 0 \end{cases}$$

4 We write $w \geqslant w'$ if $w_i \geqslant w'_i$ for each i and there exists k such that $w_k > w'_k$. w is called semi-positive if $w \geqslant \mathbf{0}$ where $\mathbf{0} = (0,\dots,0)$.

5 In order to be consistent with the definition of a DDR we have for the sake of simplicity excluded the possibility

$$\sum_{i=1}^{n} \beta_i x_i = 0$$

for some $x \in \Omega$. Otherwise we should have complicated matters, without gaining much, and define the optimal rule $\hat{\hat{f}}$

$$\hat{\hat{f}} = \begin{cases} \hat{f} & \text{if } \hat{f} \neq 0 \\ 1 & \text{otherwise} \end{cases}$$

6 Monotonicity and neutrality imply the unanimity property. A DDR is unanimous if $f(1,\dots,1) = 1$ and $f(-1,\dots,-1) = -1$. If f is neutral and monotonic but not unanimous, then either $f(1,\dots,1) = -1$ or $f(-1,\dots,-1) = 1$. By neutrality, both equations must hold, which is in contradiction to the monotonicity of f.

7 A list of all winning coalitions in proper majority games up to seven players is available in the literature on game theory. All weighted majority rules for the case $n = 6$ and $n = 7$ can be derived from the list (see, for instance, Isbell (1959)).

8 For convenience we write

$$(w \cdot x) = \sum_{i=1}^{n} w_i x_i$$

9 The detailed taxonomy of all the possibilities arising in this case is cumbersome and therefore omitted.

Chapter 3: Costs of decision rules

1 For an extensive discussion on decision-making costs see Buchanan and Tullock (1962)
2 The trade-off between k and p for given probability $\pi(p, k)$ was originally investigated by Grofman (1978). Using the normal approximation for the binomial probability, one has to solve for m using the equation

$$\frac{(p - 0.5)\sqrt{(2k + 1)}}{\sqrt{[p(1 - p)]}} = \frac{(p - 0.5 - \delta)\sqrt{[2(k + m) + 1]}}{\sqrt{[(p - \delta)(1 + \delta - p)]}}$$

where $0 \leqslant \delta < p - \frac{1}{2}$
The solution is

$$m = (k + \tfrac{1}{2}) \frac{\delta(2p - \delta - 1)}{4p(1 - p)(p - \delta - 0.5)}$$

For instance, in a committee of three members with a decisional skill of 0.8 one can obtain the same probability as in a committee of nine with a skill of 0.7.

For any given k and p the last equation allows us to investigate the substitution between m and δ. The slope of the iso-probability curves is given by

$$\left. \frac{dm}{d\delta} \right|_{\pi(p,k)=\text{const.}} = \frac{(p - 0.5)^2}{2p(1 - p)(p - 0.5 - \delta)^3}$$

3 The definition of relevance appears in Section 2.5.
4 It can easily be verified that the following is an alternative formulation of Corollary 3.4.1 (1).
The expert rule is optimal if and only if

$$p_1 > \frac{p_2 p_3}{p_2 p_3 + (1 - p_2)(1 - p_3)}$$

In other words, a necessary and sufficient condition for the superiority of the expert rule is that the probability of the expert to decide correctly is larger than the probability that the non-experts decide correctly given that they both vote unanimously.
5 Feld and Grofman (1984) have recently generalized this proposition to the case of any number of decision makers.

Chapter 5: Incomplete information on decisional skills

1 For three-member groups, however, the expert rule and simple majority rule are the only two relevant rules, see Section 2.5.
2 The human capital literature provides alternative explanations to the existence of log-normal distribution of earnings where investment and/or abilities are symmetrically distributed. Similarly, in our context, symmetric distribution of initial

individual abilities and investment in human capital may generate the log-normal distribution of individual odds of making correct judgements. In particular the product of two symmetric distributions is more positively skewed the higher the positive correlation between them (see Becker (1964, ch. 3) and Mincer (1970)).

3 Since some of the values of β_i can be negative there may exist several individuals who satisfy the condition. As long as these individuals differ in their decisional skills only one of them is the expert. If some are equally skilled the expert rule might be non-unique. Note that if μ/σ is sufficiently large then there exists at most a single individual satisfying the condition, as in such a case for any β_i, $\Pr(\beta_i \geqslant 0) \to 1$. In this case, our approximation is indeed very satisfactory. In general, then, P_e should be considered as an upper bound of the probability that the expert rule is optimal.

Chapter 6: Interdependent decisions

1 The possibility of an intentional control over the competence levels through investment in human capital is discussed in more detail in Chapter 7.
2 This statement is somewhat more general than Theorem 6.3.1 and can be proved using a similar method. The pattern (G_1, D_1) is called more independent than (G_2, D_2) if D_1 and G_1 are subsets of D_2 and G_2 respectively.
3 In the previous example we have only presented a case where $\pi(\hat{f}, p, G_0) = \pi(f^0, p, G)$.

Chapter 7: Improving decisional skills as investment in human capital

1 Alternative attempts to incorporate risk considerations into the individual's decision-making process of investment in human capital are carried out by Levhari and Weiss (1974) and Paroush (1976).
2 The concept of self-protection, in contrast to self-insurance, was introduced by Ehrlich and Becker (1972). Note that there are several other aspects of investment in human capital on both individual and social levels that are not captured by our model. For instance, the direct utility which can be drawn from the mere investment activity in human capital.
3 This h is already made beyond some past investment which was necessary for the deviation of p from $\frac{1}{2}$ and for the individual's ability of being aware of his own p. Note that we do not disregard the possibility of division of labor. The individual's ability p can be interpreted differently in different contexts. It can be either a general ability index or a specific one for particular fields. The investment in human capital h has to be given the respective meaning, e.g. general education in the first case, or specific education or on-the-job training in the second case.
4 The proofs of all propositions appear in the Appendix to Chapter 7.
5 Alternatively one can assume that the decision makers are represented not by an identical skill production function, but by a constant ability.
6 Assume that a fixed budget is available to the group and let *both* per capita investment in human capital and the number of participants in the collective decision-making process be treated as variables. If $c = 0$, then the optimum solution of the constrained optimization problem society faces is to infinitely increase k while sufficiently decreasing h.

Chapter 8: Sequential analysis: the consulting case

1 Theorem 8.2.1 provides the method for calculating π and Em.

Chapter 9: Many alternatives and mixed rules

1 A linear ordering is a complete, transitive and asymmetric relation.
2 A neutral decision rule is invariant to the labelling of the alternatives.

Chapter 10: Applications

1 Existing wisdom is replete with arguments in support of cumulative voting as an ideal elections method. As mentioned previously, advocates of this system base their arguments on the virtues of proportional representation in general, thus implying that cumulative voting is, in fact, an application of the proportional representation paragon. Other arguments emphasize the role of cumulative voting in monitoring directors' deviant conduct or ensuring free speech.

2 For example, Section 141 of the Delaware Corporation Law reads: '...(T)he vote of the majority of the directors present at a meeting...shall be the act of the board of directors unless the certificate of incorporation or by-laws shall require a vote of a greater number...'.

3 The pioneering study has been Berle and Means' (1932) classic book. The Berle and Means results (pertaining to 1929) show that in 44 percent of the 200 largest US corporations no faction of stockholders held more than a relatively small percentage of the voting stock. Those corporations were termed by the authors 'management controlled'. More recent studies show that the number of management controlled firms almost doubled in the 1960s, while the phenomenon of majority control has almost entirely vanished (Larner, 1966). For an analysis of the significance of the results of Berle and Means and of Larner, see De Alessi (1973).

4 See Section 2.2.

5 The probability of obtaining the correct decision under the simple majority rule is equal to

$$p_1p_2p_3 + p_1p_2(1-p_3) + p_1(1-p_2)p_3 + (1-p_1)p_2p_3$$
$$= 0.85 \times 0.7 \times 0.55 + 0.85 \times 0.7 \times 0.45 + 0.85 \times 0.3 \times 0.55 + 0.15 \times 0.7 \times 0.55$$
$$= 0.793$$

6 We do not make here an explicit assumption about a positive relationship between directorial stockholding and skills. A plausible argument could be made, however, that that is indeed the case. As equity holdings of a director increase, the greater is his incentive to maximize corporate profits, and the more costly his inclination to allocate corporate resources to 'personal' directorial consumption (see Jensen and Meckling (1976), and Stano (1975)).

7 See Grofman (1978).

References

Alchian, A., and H. Demsetz, 1972. 'Production, Information Costs and Economic Organization.' *American Economic Review* 62: 777–95.

Arrow, K.J. 1963. *Social Choice and Individual Values*, 2nd edition. New Haven: Yale University Press.

Barbera, S., and F. Valenciano, 1983. 'Collective Probabilistic Judgments.' *Econometrica* 51: 1033–46.

Barrett, C.R., and P.K. Pattanaik, 1983. 'Aggregation of Probabilistic Judgments.' Mimeographed.

Bartoszynski, P. 1972. 'Power Structure in Dichotomous Voting,' *Econometrica* 40: 1003–19.

Becker, G.S. 1964. *Human Capital*. New York: NBER.

Ben-Porath, Y. 1967. 'The Production of Human Capital and the Life-Cycle of Earnings.' *Journal of Political Economy* 75: 352–67.

Berle, A.A., and G.C. Means, 1932. *The Modern Corporation and Private Property*. New York: Commerce Clearing House.

Black, D. 1948. 'On the Rationale of Group Decision Making.' *Journal of Political Economy* 56: 23–34.

1958. *The Theory of Committees and Elections*. London: Cambridge University Press.

Bordley, R.F. 1982. 'A Multiplicative Formula for Aggregating Probability Assessments.' *Management Science* 28: 1137–48.

Buchanan, J., and G. Tullock 1962. *The Calculus of Consent*, Ann Arbor: University of Michigan Press.

Condorcet, N.C. de. 1785. *Essai sur l'Application de l'Analyse á la Probabilité des Decisions Rendues á la Pluraité des Voix*, Paris.

De Alessi, L. 1973. 'Private Property and Dispersion of Ownership in Large Corporations.' *Journal of Finance* 28: 839–51.

Ehrlich, I., and G.S. Becker. 1972. 'Market Insurance, Self Insurance and Self Protection.' *Journal of Political Economy* 80: 623–48.

Farquharson, R. 1969. *Theory of Voting*, New Haven: Yale University Press.

Feld, S.L., and B. Grofman. 1984. 'The Accuracy of Group Majority Decisions in Groups with Added Members.' *Public Choice* 42 (3): 273–86.

Feller, W. 1968. *An Introduction to Probability Theory and Its Applications, Vol. 1*. New York: Wiley.

Fishburn, P.D. 1973. *The Theory of Social Choice*. Princeton: Princeton University Press.

Fishburn, P.D., and W.V. Gehrlein, 1977*a*. 'Towards a Theory of Elections with Probabilistic Voting.' *Econometrica* 45: 1907–23.

1977*b*. 'Collective Rationality versus Distribution of Power of Binary Social Choice Functions.' *Journal of Economic Theory* 15: 72–91.

Gelfand, A., and H. Solomon. 1973. 'A Study of Poisson's Models for Jury Verdicts in Criminal and Civil Trials.' *Journal of American Statistical Association* 68: 271–8.

1975. 'Analyzing the Decision-Making Process of the American Jury.' *Journal of the American Statistical Association* 70: 305–10.

Grofman, B. 1975. 'A Comment on "Democratic Theory: A Preliminary Mathematical Model"'. *Public Choice* 21: 100–3.

1978. 'Judgemental Competence of Individuals and Groups in a Dichotomous Choice Situation: Is a Majority of Heads Better than One?' *Journal of Mathematical Sociology* 6: 47–60.

Grofman, B., G. Owen, and S. Feld, 1983. 'Thirteen Theorems in Search of the Truth.' *Theory and Decision* 15: 261–78.

Isbell, S.R. 1959. 'On the Enumeration of Majority Games.' *Mathematical Tables and Other Aids of Computation* 13: 21–8.

Jensen, M.C., and W.H. Meckling. 1976. 'Theory of the Firm: Managerial Behavior. Agency Costs and Ownership Structure.' *Journal of Financial Economics* 3: 305–60.

Klevorick, A.K., and M. Rothschild. 1979. 'A Model of the Jury Decision Process.' *Journal of Legal Studies* 8: 141–64.

Larner, R.J. 1966. 'Ownership and Control in the 200 Largest Nonfinancial Corporations, 1929–1963.' *American Economic Review* 56: 777–87.

Lehman, E.L. 1959. *Testing Statistical Hypotheses*. New York: Wiley.

Leibowitz, A., and R. Tollison, 1980. 'Free Riding, Shirking, and Team Production in Legal Partnerships.' *Economic Inquiry* 18: 380–94.

Levhari, D., and Weiss, Y. 1974. 'The Effect of Risk on Investment in Human Capital.' *The American Economic Review* 64: 950–63.

Luce, R.D. 1959. *Individual Choice Behavior*. New York: Wiley.

Madansky, A. 1978. 'Externally Bayesian Groups.' Reprint, Center for Management of Public and Nonprofit Enterprise, University of Chicago.

Marshack, J., and R. Radner, 1972. *Economic Theory of Teams*. New Haven: Yale University Press.

May, K.O. 1952. 'A Set of Independent Necessary and Sufficient Conditions for Simple Majority Decision'. *Econometrica* 20: 680–4.

McCall, J.J. 1970. 'Economics of Information and Job Search.' *Quarterly Journal of Economics* 90: 113–26.

Mill, J.S. 1861. *Considerations on Representative Government*. London: Parker, Son and Brown.

Mincer, J. 1970. 'The Distribution of Labor Incomes: A Survey with Special Reference to the Human Capital Approach.' *Journal of Economic Literature* 7: 1–26.

1974. *Schooling. Experience and Earnings*. New York: NBER.

Morris, P.A. 1974. 'Decision Analysis Expert Use.' *Management Science* 20: 1233–41.

1977. 'Combining Expert Judgments. A Bayesian Approach.' *Management Science* 23: 679–93.

1983. 'An Axiomatic Approach to Expert Resolution.' *Management Science* 29: 24–32.

Mortenson, Dale T. 1970. 'Job Search, The Duration of Unemployment and the Phillips Curve.' *American Economic Review* 60: 847–62.

Nitzan, S., and J. Paroush. 1980. 'Investment in Human Capital and Social Self Protection Under Uncertainty.' *International Economic Review* 21: 547–57.

1981. 'The Characterization of Decisive Weighted Majority Rules.' *Economics Letters* 7: 119–24.

1982. 'Optimal Decision Rules in Uncertain Dichotomous Choice Situations.' *International Economic Review* 23: 289–97.

1983. 'Small Panels of Experts in Dichotomous Choice Situations.' *Decision Sciences* 14 (3): 314–25. (Published by the American Institute for Dicision Sciences.)

1984a. 'Potential Variability of Decisional Skills in Uncertain Dichotomous Choice Situations.' *Mathematical Social Sciences* 8: 217–27.

1984b. 'Are Qualified Majority Rules Special?' *Public Choice* 42: 257–72.

1984c. 'The Significance of Independent Voting Under Uncertain Dichotomous Choice Situations.' *Theory and Decision* 17 (1): 47–60. (Copyright © 1984 by D. Reidel Publishing Company, Dordrecht, Holland.)

1984d. 'A General Theorem and Eight Corollaries in Search of a Correct Decision.' *Theory and Decision* 17: 211–20. (Copyright © 1984 by D. Reidel Publishing Company, Dordrecht, Holland.)

1984e. 'Partial Information on Decisional Skills and the Desirability of the Expert Rule in Uncertain Dichotomous Choice Situations. *Theory and Decision* 17: 275–86. (Copyright © 1984 by D. Reidel Publishing Company, Dordrecht, Holland.)

Nitzan, S. and U. Procaccia. 1982. 'Cumulative Voting for Directors.' mimeographed.

Paroush, J. 1974. 'Investment Policy Under Uncertainty: The Case of Search in a Multi-Market Situation.' *Southern Economic Journal* 40: 397–403.

1976. 'The Risk Effect and Investment in Human Capital.' *European Economic Review* 8: 339–47.

1981. 'Market Research as Self Protection of Competitive Firm Under Price Uncertainty.' *International Economic Review* 22: 365–75.

1985. 'Notes on Partnerships in The Services Sector.' *Journal of Economic Behaviour and Organization* 6: 79–87.

Paroush, J., and Y.C. Peles. 1978 'Search for Information and Portfolio Selection.' *Journal of Banking and Finance* 2: 163–77.

Poisson, S.D. 1837 *Recherches sur la Probabilité des Jugements en Matière Criminelle et en Matière Civile.* Procedees des Règles Générales du Calcul des Probabilités. Bachelier. Imprimateur Libraire, Paris.

Rae, D.W. 1969. 'Decision Rules and Individual Values in Constitutional Choice.' *American Political Science Review* 63: 40–63.

Schofield, N.J. 1972. 'Is Majority Rule Special?' In: *Probability Models of Collective Decision Making*, edited by R.G. Niemi and H.F. Weisberg. Columbus, Ohio: Merill.

Sen, A.K. 1970. *Collective Choice and Social Welfare*, San Francisco: Holden Day.

1977, 'Social Choice Theory: A Re-Examination.' *Econometrica* 45: 53–89.

Stano, M. 1975. 'Executive ownership Interests and Corporate Performance.' *Southern Economic Journal* 42: 272–8.

Stein, C.M. 1946. 'A Note on Cumulative Sums.' *Annals of Mathematical Statistics* 17: 189–99.

Stigler, G. 1961. 'The Economics of Information.' *Journal of Political Economy* 69: 213–25.

Straffin, Jr., P.D. 1977. 'Majority Rule and General Decision Rules.' *Theory and Decision* 8: 351–60

Wald, A. 1947. *Sequential Analysis.* New York: Wiley.

Young, P. 1983. 'Ranking and Choice: An Axiomatic Approach to Maximum Likelihood Methods.' Mimeographed. Presented at the Pooling of Information Conference, University of California, Irvine, California.

Zeckhauser, R. 1969. 'Majority Rule With Lotteries on Alternatives.' *Quarterly Journal of Economics* 83: 696–703.

Index